TIM SHENTON

D1647233

Forgotten heroes
of revival

Great men of the 18th century evangelical awakening

DayOne

© Day One Publications 2004

First printed 2004

ISBN 1 903087 70-8

9 781903 087701

British Library Cataloguing in Publication Data available

Published by Day One Publications
Ryelands Road, Leominster, HR6 8NZ
☎ 01568 613 740 FAX 01568 611 473
email—sales@dayone.co.uk
web site—www.dayone.co.uk
North American—e-mail—sales@dayonebookstore.com
North American web site—www.dayonebookstore.com

Designed by Steve Devane and printed by CPD

Contents

PREFACE **5**

1 GEORGE THOMSON (1698–1782) *GOD'S PIONEER IN CORNWALL* **8**

2 JAMES ROUQUET (1730–1776) *THE POOR MAN'S PREACHER* **32**

3 CAPTAIN JONATHAN SCOTT (1735–1807) *IN THE LORD'S ARMY* **62**

4 DAVID SIMPSON (1744–1799) *THE GOOD SAMARITAN* **90**

5 THOMAS PENTYCROSS (1748–1808) *FAITHFUL TO ONE CAUSE* **166**

INDEX **190**

Dedication

Thanks, Tim

'God is not unjust; he will not forget your work and the love you have shown him as you have helped his people and continue to help them.' (Hebrews 6:10).

Not long ago a visiting preacher came to my church, whose job it was to train men for the ministry, and part of his time was spent teaching them how to preach effectively. He was a well respected minister, who was noted for his orthodox theology. On this particular morning he preached an evangelically 'sound' sermon, with three well constructed, clear and relevant points. What he said was interesting and no doubt some in the congregation were edified. I imagine, as he stood at the door after the service, many thanked him for a 'good word'.

I cannot say what the speaker thought of his own message, but I remember thinking to myself that there was a vital ingredient missing in the sermon and in the preacher—passion! There was no passion in what he said, no fire burning in his heart or in the words he so carefully uttered. What he said could not be criticised theologically, but it lacked the 'life, fire, wing and force' that characterised the sermons of men like George Whitefield. Martyn Lloyd-Jones described preaching as 'logic on fire', but on that morning I felt none of the glowing fervour that emanates from truly great men.

Although the five men in this book were notably different in personality and performance, they were one in purpose and passion. Their deep love for Christ and for the souls of sinners enabled them to stand strong through the storms of persecution, and to preach a message that fed not just the mind with theology and high ideals, but reached into and captivated the heart. In short, the word of life they proclaimed shook their congregations—it stirred them, stunned them, saved them—and though many did not agree with what they heard, they could not deny that here were men in love with Jesus and earnest in their desire to save souls.

I once heard a man preach with such passion that afterwards a member of the congregation said, 'I didn't agree with a word he said, but I loved watching him worship God as he said it.' The gospel is not a dry and barren desert, suitable only for intellectuals, it is life and power! 'I am not ashamed of the gospel,' declares the apostle Paul, 'because it is the power of God for the salvation of everyone who believes' (Romans 1:16). In this day and age we need men to return to a simple child-like faith in the true gospel, men who are constrained by God's Spirit, whose hearts are on fire for Christ, and who will lay down their lives for the kingdom of heaven. We need men of love and truth and life in our pulpits.

Thomson, Rouquet, Scott, Simpson and Pentycross are five men who loved Jesus. They knew what he had done for them and had been gripped and challenged by the message of salvation—that was the motivation behind their ministries and why they discharged their callings so faithfully. They were prepared, whatever the cost, to obey the command of their captain, 'Go and make disciples of all nations', and to 'spend and be spent' for the benefit of others. They might not be in the top ten of great preachers, but their lives were dedicated to serve God and they played an important role in the eighteenth century revival in England; therefore they must not be forgotten.

Acknowledgement and Dedication

I would like to express my sincere thanks to Tim Brinton of Macclesfield, whose constant support and encouragement with David Simpson have been inspirational. Not only is he knowledgeable on Simpson, but he was prepared to spend a considerable amount of time gathering and collating material for me, reading through and commenting on my MS, and assisting me, with an unbounded enthusiasm, in whatever way he could. I am deeply appreciative of his help and it is to him I dedicate this book.

Tim Shenton

George Thomson

God's pioneer in Cornwall

George Thomson has been rightly called the predecessor of all the evangelical fathers in England. A year or two before George Whitefield's conversion and some ten years before the Wesleys began their now famous visits to Cornwall, Thomson was conducting an evangelical ministry among his people at St Gennys, a windswept village on the top of the cliffs overlooking the Atlantic in the north of the county. John Bennet, a neighbouring curate in charge of the isolated parishes of North Tamerton (about twelve miles from St Gennys), Laneast and Tresmere, was converted through Thomson's ministry in 1742, and the more illustrious Samuel Walker of Truro did not embrace evangelicalism until 1747.

Thomson is thought to have descended from the 'good Devonshire family' of John Thompson, Lord Haversham, whose daughter was a countess of Anglesey. (In the St Gennys registers George always omits the letter 'p' when signing his name.) He was born at Fremington, near Barnstaple early in 1698, and was baptised on 1 March. Through his mother the family inherited the Colybeare estates. His father, an enlightened and earnest Protestant, was a merchant trading with Spain, where he had lived for some years. Knowledge that he possessed a Spanish Bible led to a diligent search of his house by members of the Inquisition.

They entered the house in form; they went, to the best of their knowledge, into every room, below and above, but could find no such thing: for it happened, that in one parlour, there was, opposite to the door by which they went in, another door leading into another parlour, in which the Spanish Bible lay upon the table: but this door, as the Lord would have it … entirely escaped their notice. Nor could any other reason of this be assigned, nor any other account of it given, as the gentleman himself observed, but that his God blinded their eyes, in this single case, that they *could* not see. A happy circumstance for him! on which he reflected, with gratitude, thankfulness and praise.[1]

After this narrow escape, John took the first opportunity to leave Spain and

St Gennys vicarage

return to England, living for some years in London, before settling in Brynsworthy (two miles from Barnstaple), where he

… happily spent his time with his family in reading, in acts of true devotion, in playing on instruments of music, and in instilling gospel truths, the grand peculiarities of divine revelation, into the young, ductile minds of his children, watering these pious efforts with fervent prayers. By which means, through the blessing of God, was laid … in [George] the foundation of those principles of divine truth, of that faith, zeal, integrity and holiness, which afterwards so eminently shone forth in him.[2]

Apart from the religious education he received from his father, little is known about Thomson's early years. At the age of ten he experienced some serious spiritual impressions, but they were transient and soon disappeared. At school and university he did not participate in any open sin or flagrant vice, but lived in that carelessness of spirit and worldly-mindedness that is common among those who only have a show of religion. On 17 February 1716, at the age of eighteen, he matriculated at Exeter College, Oxford, where his father sent him to prepare for the ministry, and nearly four years later he took his Bachelor of Civil Law degree. He was ordained deacon on 1 July 1722 by the Bishop of Exeter, and the following day licensed to the curacy of Jacobstow in north Cornwall, where he stayed until after his ordination to the priesthood four years later.

At an unknown date he became chaplain of the *Tiger*, a man-of-war bound for America, an appointment he exchanged for a similar position in the army as chaplain to the Fortieth Regiment of Foot. He was presented to the benefice of St Gennys, which was close to his former curacy, on 10 September 1732, on the introduction of Sir John Molesworth of Pencarrow and James Eliot, a kinsman from Port Eliot. He moved into a six-roomed vicarage that was built of 'stone, mud and rags' in a position 'sheltered amidst grounds which commanded a noble view'. James Hervey, on one of his visits, described it as 'on rising ground upon the edge of the ocean, whence I have daily prospect of the works of the Lord and his wonders in the deep'.[3] Not satisfied with its dilapidated condition, Thomson rebuilt it in 1734. Money was not a problem as he had an annual private income of £500 from the family estate.

Initially at St Gennys he was a happy and lively young vicar, whose company neighbouring ministers, gentry and ordinary folk enjoyed. Philip Doddridge, who was familiar with the circumstances of his life, likened him to the early character of Colonel Gardiner. He was regarded as a 'first rate genius', with few Christian morals, whose preaching had little or no effect for good on his parishioners. After he had been there about two years, probably in 1734, he was shaken out of his careless lifestyle by a dream, which was repeated three times in one night, with increasing terrors. In the dream he was warned, 'This day [in a] month, at six in the afternoon, you must appear before the judgement seat of Christ, to give an account of the dreadful abuse of all your talents, and the injuries done [to] the souls committed to your care.' He was so alarmed that he awoke in great amazement, but soon, in order to ease his conscience, thought, 'Glad I am it was no more than a dream; I am no old woman to mind dreams; I will sleep again.'[4]

He went back to sleep, although somewhat disturbed in his mind, and the same dream was repeated, 'with greater circumstances of terror'. He awoke again in deep distress, but after 'various tossings and agitation of mind' he once more fell asleep. The dream was again repeated, 'with still more terrible circumstances'. This time he awoke and could not get back to sleep. He was as convinced that he was going to die at the set hour as 'a condemned criminal of the day set by the judge for his execution'.

In a state of panic and horror, he called together his friends, and the more prominent members of his parish, and explained to them his dream. He begged them to supply the parish with another minister, who could fulfil his duties, and to return to him in a month on the predicted day of his death. To this they agreed. In the meantime, Thomson shut himself away with his Bible in an attempt to find peace of mind, but instead of being comforted by the Scriptures, he read nothing but words of condemnation. He reasoned that it was 'not consistent with the honour of God, as supreme Governor, to pardon so great an offender, who had brought so great and public dishonour to his holy name'.

After a fortnight of increasing distress, he turned to Romans 3:26: 'To declare I say at this time his righteousness, that he might be just, and the justifier of him which believeth in Jesus.' As he read the verse his fears of condemnation gradually turned to the hope of eternal life. He saw that God 'could be glorified in his salvation, through the propitiation of Christ's most precious blood'. The scales fell from his eyes and he understood for the first time the redemptive work of Christ, which was to become the foundation of his spiritual awakening and evangelical ministry. He remained in 'unassisted solitude' in 'an obscure parsonage of the west' and became increasingly convinced of the doctrines of salvation through faith alone, doctrines that the Wesleys did not grasp for another five or six years.

However, he did not expect to escape the sentence of death that had been repeated in his dreams. The dreaded day arrived, his friends returned, and the clock struck six. Nothing happened. He was still alive. His friends congratulated him and he understood the mystery of the divine warning.

His soul was filled with a burning zeal for the honour of God and with love to precious souls. He returned to the pulpit, preached experimentally man's fall, sin and misery; the necessity of regeneration; the imputation of Christ's righteousness; the necessity of holiness as the evidence of acceptance before a holy God, and the absolute need of the energy of the Holy Spirit to begin and carry on a saving change in heart and life. The hand of the Lord remarkably sealed the above doctrines in the conversion of numbers in his parish.[5]

Samuel Furly, in the preface to *Original Sacred Hymns*, says, 'Now zeal, not malignant, but true, love sincere and fervent, concern for the souls of sinners unfeigned, and deep desire to promote the glory of God strong and ardent, accompanied with humility and undissembled and profound, urged him forward to extraordinary labours in the holy employment of his particular office.'[6]

By 1736 Thomson was acquainted with other awakened men. In January of that year he wrote to Isaac Watts, in his eyes the spiritual father of the times, stating that, though unknown to him, he would value his prayers and in return pray for him. The letter, fervid and overflowing in tone, is the only production of Thomson's pen extant, so we quote it in full.

St Ginnys, Jan. 17, 1736.

Poet, Divine, Saint, the delight, the guide, the wonder of the virtuous world; permit, Rev. Sir, a stranger unknown, and likely to be for ever unknown to desire one blessing from you in a private way. 'Tis this, that when you approach the throne of grace, and lift up holy hands, when you get closest to the mercy-seat, and wrestle mightily for the peace of *Jerusalem,* you would breathe one petition for my soul's health. In return I promise you a share for life in my unworthy prayers, who honour you as a father and a brother (though differently ordered) and conclude myself,

Your affectionate humble servant,
GEORGE THOMSON.

PS If you can forgive my freedom, and find a few minutes leisure to ascertain me of your kind design to oblige, to make me happy direct to *George Thomson* vicar of *St Ginny's,* near *Camelford,* in *Cornwall.*7

Isaac Watts

Two years later James Hervey was in Devon, where he had been sent to convalesce after a serious illness. He stayed with the Orchards at Stoke Abbey. Thomson knew the Orchards well and his road to Brynsworthy passed by their mansion. In 1739 Hervey supplied for Thomson's flock at St Gennys for six weeks in his absence. After his return to Stoke Abbey, he wrote to George Whitefield in his usual humble spirit, 'O that he [Thomson] may not find his dear flock gone back, but adorned in Christian knowledge, during his absence from them.'8 Hervey was ordained priest at Exeter in December of that year and for some time worked as curate at Bideford until he was dismissed by the rector in 1743 for his evangelical views. During this time he and Thomson became the best of friends and were always welcomed by each other's converts.

Later Hervey wrote to his former parishioners in the religious society at Bideford strongly recommending Thomson.

I rejoice to hear that dear Mr Thompson proposes to make you a monthly visit. O that his doctrine may distil as the dew! He will teach you the way of God more perfectly, for he has the unction of the Holy One and knows the truth as it is in Jesus. There will not be wanting those who will censure his righteous dealings, and ridicule his zeal for the glorious Redeemer; but all those who have Jesus and his salvation, will say, 'The Lord prosper you!'[9]

While in Devon, Hervey planned and probably started to write his *Meditations among the Tombs,* which was inspired by his wanderings in Kilkhampton churchyard, where he sat among the tombs, reading the epitaphs on the headstones. After this volume was published, which he had dedicated to his friend's eldest daughter, 'Miss R.', who must have been very young,[10] he wrote to Thomson on 28 June 1746, a letter that underlines their intimacy.

I presume this will find you at Brynsworthy, that agreeable seat, where, three years ago, I passed several delightful weeks [with the Thomsons]. Oh! when shall I spend my hours of conversation so much to my improvement! …

If, at some leisure moment, you should happen to cast a glance upon the lines [of *Meditations among the Tombs*], mark, dear sir, their blemishes, correct their improprieties, and improve them into a greater neatness, in case a second edition should be demanded …

Be pleased to make my most respectful and affectionate compliments acceptable to Mrs Thompson. I wish Miss Thompson may be a living picture of that amiable and virtuous woman, whose price is above rubies. If your trusty friend, Mr B[ennet] is with you, pray tell him I love him, because he loves Mr Thompson …

Let it not be long before dear Mr Thompson, with a letter, delights, animates and comforts his most obliged and affectionate friend,

JAMES HERVEY.[11]

Hervey always thought very highly of Thomson, describing him as

… unfurling the gospel standard with a tongue touched from the heavenly altar, pleading with his people not to follow the wiles of Satan and lean on his broken reeds but to build their faith on the Rock of Ages. He preached to his flock as the ruined and undone sinners they were, showing how God's mighty arm was still strong to save them from their plight. His message was always: 'They who know Christ's free goodness, will put their whole trust in him, and seek no other way to the father of mercy but through his merit.'[12]

About 1740 Thomson, who married four times in seventeen years, married Grace Trevanion, a daughter of Sir Nicholas Trevanion. After her death he married Rebecca Dingley, who also died unexpectedly. It was probably to Rebecca that Hervey was referring when he wrote his last letter from Bideford on 5 April 1743 to Mrs Orchard, reporting what he had observed on a recent visit to St Gennys, 'My dear friend Mr Thomson has found an amiable partner. Love has joined their hearts, religion has harmonised their tempers, and Providence mixes blessings with their bands: they really live together as "heirs together of the grace of life".'[13] Next Thomson married Penelope Lucas, and finally, in 1757, Honor Eliot, probably his first cousin, and said to be connected with the Eliots of Port Eliot, the elder branch of which now takes the title of Earl of St Germans. Honor was a pious and amiable woman, who survived her husband by five years, dying at Bideford in 1787. She was buried with him at Barnstaple.

James Hervey

In 1738 Thomson subscribed £6 19s to George Whitefield, who was about to leave for Georgia. The following year they met in Bath, and Tyerman in his *Life of Whitefield*, referring to this meeting, says that Thomson was 'from the first a hearty friend of the Oxford Methodists'.[14] Whitefield first visited Cornwall in 1743, where he met not only Thomson, but John Bennet, a 'clergyman about eighty years of age, but not above one year old in the school of Christ. He lately preached three times, and rode forty miles the same day ... I cannot well describe with what power the word was attended ... The old clergyman was much broken.'[15] According to Charles Wesley, Bennet had 'received the kingdom as a little child' upon

Thomson's preaching 'salvation by faith', and had ever since 'owned the truth and its followers'.[16]

On Saturday 12 November, Whitefield accompanied Thomson to his vicarage at St Gennys, where he stayed about two weeks and was the first to preach in his friend's pulpit.

I am glad that the Lord inclined my heart to come hither [Whitefield wrote on 25 November]. He has been with us of a truth. How did his stately steps appear in the sanctuary last Lord's Day! Many, many prayers were put up by the worthy rector and others for an outpouring of God's blessed Spirit. They were answered. Arrows of conviction flew so thick and so fast, and such a universal weeping prevailed from one end of the congregation to the other, that good Mr Thompson could not help going from seat to seat, to encourage and comfort the wounded souls.[17]

Thomson and Whitefield took to each other immediately, being kindred spirits—'warm, emotional and demonstrative'.

On 15 July 1744 Charles Wesley travelled to St Gennys, 'where our loving host and brother Thomson received us with open arms'. The following day Thomson read prayers at Bennet's church and Wesley preached on 'Fear not, little flock'. On 2 August Thomson accompanied Wesley to Penryn, where he preached to two thousand people. Three days later Wesley preached at Gwennap for over two hours to a large and deeply affected congregation. 'My brother Thomson was astonished,' reported Wesley, 'and confessed he had never seen the like among Germans, predestinarians, or any others.' When he preached in Bennet's church the next day 'against harmless diversions', he exclaimed, 'By harmless diversions I was kept asleep in the devil's arms, secure in a state of damnation for eighteen years.' No sooner were the words uttered than John Meriton added aloud, 'And I for twenty-five!' 'And I,' cried Thomson, 'for

Charles Wesley

thirty-five!' 'And I,' joined in Bennet, 'for above seventy.'[18] Thomson evidently followed Wesley to Bath, for the latter's journal for 16 September states, 'My brother Thomson assisted in administering; and was, as he expressed it, on the highest round of Jacob's ladder.'

During this time Thomson preached twice every Lord's Day at St Gennys, which had a population of eighty families, none of whom were dissenters, and often on other days when he could gather his people together. The average number of communicants was seventy. In Lent he catechised all that were sent, but sadly few attended, and occasionally he preached in other churches, which aroused the hostility of neighbouring clergymen, who named his followers 'Methodists', a derogatory term for anyone who was earnest about religion.

John Cory, the incumbent of Marhamchurch, bitterly disapproved of Thomson's work. In his return of 1745 to Bishop Claggett, he wrote that there were no dissenters in his parish, 'but only one family whom I am informed frequent Mr Thompson's irregular meetings and accompany him on his circumforaneous vociferations. There is no licensed meeting house in the parish nor any who take it upon them to teach unless in the said family where (I have been told) some of those deluded people who style themselves Methodists, Thompson's and Bennet's followers, who meet together in private.' William Leaver of Kilkhampton complained that in his parish there were sixteen dissenters, 'who called themselves Methodists' and their leader was George Thomson; while Thomas Serle of Treneglos and Warbstow said there were no dissenters in his parish 'unless they may be called dissenters who go by the name of Methodist—a set of people who are chiefly encouraged and abetted by a neighbouring clergyman'.[19] From these comments it is clear that many in the Church regarded Thomson and Bennet as the real leaders of Methodism in Cornwall.

However, Thomson was not to be stopped in his work by the murmurings of unenlightened clergy. In the summer of 1745 he welcomed John Wesley, who preached in St Gennys on 16 June to a group of 'serious hearers, but few of them appeared to feel what they heard'.[20] He preached again on Monday, when many assented to and approved of the truth. On Wednesday Thomson followed Wesley to the western part of Cornwall, where they visited St Michael's Mount and the St Ives region. At Redruth they heard that Thomas

Thomas Maxfield

Maxfield had been seized for the army at Crowan, so they quickly rode to the rescue, but on the way received information that he had been removed the night before. They eventually found him at the house of Henry Tomkins. On leaving they were met by a mob of forty or fifty ruffians, who started to throw stones at them, one of which struck Thomson's servant. The next day they rode to Marazion in an effort to help Maxfield, but unfortunately were not successful. After accompanying Wesley on his preaching tour for a further week, Thomson returned home on the 28th.

Thomson's support for the Wesleys, his own itinerations, particularly at Bennet's churches, and the complaints of neighbouring clergy, caused Bishop Nicholas Claggett to summon Thomson to Exeter in the summer of 1746 'to give an account of his behaviour and zeal'. Claggett admonished Thomson and advised him to confine his preaching to his own parish under the pain of episcopal displeasure. Thomson's defiant response to this censure was to welcome Charles Wesley to Cornwall not long after. Wesley preached at St Gennys morning and evening on 24 August, which is the last record of these two friends meeting in the county.

Three weeks later Thomson joined John Wesley at Week St Mary after losing his way on the moorland tracks. He again opened his church to him in 1747 and 1748, when on 18 September Wesley preached to an attentive congregation. 'I question if there were more than two persons in the congregation who did not take it to themselves,' he remarked. 'Old Mrs T[homson] did, who was in tears during a great part of the sermon. And so did Mr B[ennet], who afterwards spoke of himself in such a manner as I rejoiced to hear.'[21] The following year Thomson visited Charles Wesley in London and heard him preach powerfully early in the morning. During the sacrament Thomson cried out to Wesley, 'This is heaven! I could not bear any more.'

Thomson also received encouragement from other quarters. Writing in

1747, Doddridge expressed the hope that an account of Thomson's conversion would be made public 'whenever the established Church of England shall lose one of its brightest living ornaments, and one of the most useful members which that, or perhaps any other Christian communion can boast; in the meantime, may his exemplary life be long continued, and his zealous ministry abundantly prospered!'[22] High praise indeed from such a great man. Writing to Thomson on 6 July 1747 and speaking for his wife and himself, Doddridge said that he 'can never reflect on the hours we spent with you at [Bath in June 1746], without much pleasure'. He would gladly correspond with Thomson on a weekly basis.

Philip Doddridge

In 1747 Claggett was succeeded by the notorious George Lavington, whose antipathy for anything 'Methodist' is almost legendary. Lavington soon had an opportunity to challenge Thomson. In March 1748 all the neighbouring ministers shut their pulpit doors against Thomson, including the vicar of Tawstock, Charles Hill, 'a pious and exemplary minister' and an old friend from whom Thomson had expected support. Part of Thomson's estate was in Hill's parish, so on the next occasion he travelled there, he thought to himself, 'My old friend Mr Hill has not been kind; but when I consider what my God, in Christ, has forgiven me since I was last in his parish, ought not I to forgive all his injuries to me? I will try to imitate my great forgiver. I will go and visit Mr Hill.' As soon as Hill saw Thomson all his resentments melted away. He ran to meet him, embraced him, and said, 'O my dear brother Thomson, your kindness has overcome me; will you preach for me next Lord's Day?' 'With all my heart, brother Hill,' replied Thomson, 'on the first opportunity, but cannot next Lord's Day, because I have made no provision for my own people.'[23] Hill continued to implore his help, but could not persuade Thomson to change his mind. After two hours of stimulating conversation, they parted.

Soon after Thomson had left, Hill was so severely afflicted that he was unable to go into his pulpit to preach. He quickly wrote to Thomson and sent the letter by a special messenger, who overtook Thomson on the road. Thomson read the letter and without a moment's hesitation told the messenger to return to his master and report that he would hurry home, provide a supply for his own parish and, by the will of God, return and take his place on the next Sabbath. Thomson did return to preach in Hill's pulpit, but his friend could not attend the service.

However, his son, then a student at Oxford and home for the vacation, heard him and was so 'effectually reached' that when Thomson had pronounced the blessing in the afternoon, he stood up and begged the congregation to stop for a few minutes and listen to what he had to say.

You may well wonder at my desiring you to stop [said young Hill], as I myself have reason to wonder at the reason of it. Know then, that the dear man that sits in the pulpit, has not only said, but proved, that nothing done by, or wrought in the sinful race of Adam, can be the ground of their acceptance before a holy God; that Christ's blood is the only propitiation; his obedience and satisfaction, the only ground of acceptance—this doctrine I now believe. I now feel the power of working love and obedience to God in Christ, and I desired you to stop, that I might recommend the doctrine to all of you who thus have heard it.[24]

He then sat down, with tears streaming down his face.

For some considerable time, young Hill was overcome by redeeming love, until Satan attempted to destroy his new faith. He was so strongly opposed for his beliefs that he suffered a form of religious melancholia. He became delirious and endured dreadful temptations, so that at times he uttered blasphemies, though formerly, even before his conversion, he had hated all open profaneness. Neighbouring ministers were quick to inform Bishop Lavington that Thomson's ministry had turned an amiable youth into a madman. Lavington of course joined in these accusations, much to Thomson's distress. After pouring out his heart before God, Thomson applied to Doddridge for advice. The latter was deeply affected by the news and in his reply foretold Hill's restoration.

How long Hill suffered in the above manner is unknown, but by 1750 he had fully recovered and was continuing his studies at Oxford. Some time later he was ordained to the ministry and 'proved both a Boanerges for awakening sinners, and a Barnabas to saints'.[25]

News of Thomson's other 'irregularities' soon reached Lavington, including his ministry at a nonconformist place of worship. The bishop, angered by Thomson's 'Methodism', summoned him to Launceston on 24 July 1749 and charged him 'with having preached in parishes not belonging to him, and at unlicensed places'. Thomson admitted the truth of the charges. He was then admonished and told to restrict his preaching to his own parish church 'under pain of ecclesiastical censures'. Then Lavington, in his typically aggressive style, threatened him that if he continued his irregularities, he would be defrocked. Thomson's reaction was to take off his gown, throw it at the bishop's feet, and declare, 'I can preach the gospel without a gown,' and storm off. Lavington, shocked at Thomson's audacity, immediately sent for him and tried hard to pacify him.

With this example of Thomson's 'holy boldness', it is easy to see why Balleine calls him 'a firebrand of the Berridge type'.[26] Hole, in his *Biographical Sketches*, makes the following comment on Thomson's behaviour:

We cannot but think, and we repeat it, that this excellent man was not acting as became a beneficed clergyman in those critical times; that yielding to his natural warmth he sought to pursue a lesser good in one direction without sufficiently considering a wider ultimate good in another; that he was increasing the difficulties of those few brethren who, like Walker in his own county, were no less than himself zealously labouring to promote a revival in the Church, but in the spirit of conciliation and order.[27]

Ignoring Lavington's threat, Thomson again welcomed John Wesley, who preached at St Gennys on 26 August 'with little effect',[28] and George Whitefield to Cornwall in 1750. He met Whitefield at Plymouth in March before returning with him to St Gennys, where he preached at the Sunday service. Whitefield described that Sabbath as 'a glorious day of the Son of Man'. Both men then embarked on a tour of west Cornwall, visiting such places as Redruth and St Ives and receiving great encouragement. Whitefield was obviously impressed with Thomson and reported that he was 'mighty hearty, and is gone to his parish in a gospel flame'.[29] A few days

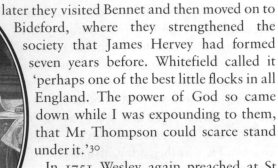

George Whitefield

later they visited Bennet and then moved on to Bideford, where they strengthened the society that James Hervey had formed seven years before. Whitefield called it 'perhaps one of the best little flocks in all England. The power of God so came down while I was expounding to them, that Mr Thompson could scarce stand under it.'[30]

In 1751 Wesley again preached at St Gennys and two years later he comments that he 'never saw so many people' in the church, 'nor did I ever before speak so plainly to them. They hear, but when will they feel? O what can man do towards raising either dead bodies or dead souls!'[31] Perhaps Wesley's doctrinal opinions produced this 'unfeeling' reaction to his sermon, and perhaps he took their coolness personally, for he never preached at St Gennys again. Some think a rift developed between the two men because Thomson joined the Moravian society *Unitas Fratrum*, whose views were 'a little fantastic, seducing many Methodist converts, and occasioning now and then morbid seclusion or even secession among clergymen'.[32]

It is more likely that Thomson's fervent Calvinistic outlook caused Wesley uneasiness, for Thomson was never afraid of declaring his views in a forthright manner, even on controversial issues. His Calvinistic views are clearly seen in the book of 226 hymns he wrote, and which was edited by Samuel Furly, rector of Roche in Cornwall. Thomson's insistence on 'free grace', 'God's free choice from all eternity', and other cardinal Calvinistic doctrines appear throughout. The following example will suffice:

Believers would ye gladly know,
Why some the gospel net confine,
Whilst over others clear they go;
The reason is the will divine.

Seek ye to know why some can melt,
Beneath the word, and some are stone;
The cause why 'tis, and 'tis not felt,
Lies in Jehovah's breast alone.

He makes the hearts of some to flow,
As wax the gospel melts them down;
Yet others more obdurate grow,
Like clay, more harden'd by the sun.

Then n'er let us his will dispute,
Nor foolishly his ways arraign,
Before their God let men be mute,
'Tis fit and right that he should reign.[33]

Many of the early evangelicals were moderate Calvinists, whereas Thomson, while not intolerant of others, was sterner and more unbending in his views. As time went on the doctrines of Whitefield appealed to him much more than the Arminianism of Wesley. In one of his hymns he writes about Whitefield's return to England from America with great enthusiasm:

Now for our WHITEFIELD's safe return,
Let us our God adore;
A thousand hearts exult and burn,
To hear he's come once more.[34]

In his younger days Thomson played various musical instruments, which may have helped him to express his evangelical thoughts in *Original Sacred Hymns*, a work in which 'a pretty poetical talent sometimes shines through' a 'native, artless simplicity'.[35] His aim, however, was not to please the ear, but to awaken the conscience, instruct the mind, and comfort the heart. Sometimes, in a single hymn, he furnishes the mind with many edifying thoughts. Thomson never intended them for the public, and only agreed on publication if his name was not included. In the preface, the editor Samuel Furly, comments,

ORIGINAL

Sacred Hymns,

With a PREFACE,

CONTAINING

Some ACCOUNT of the

AUTHOR

Quid abdicatas, in meam curam, pater,
Redire musas præcipis?
Negant camœnis, nec patent Appolini
Dicata Christo pectora.

Nunc alia mentem vis agit, major Deus,
Aliosque mores postulat.

Paulin.

Quos si tranquilla studeas cognoscere cura,
Tutus ab adverso turbine, Lector, eris.

Prosp.

Speaking to yourselves in Psalms, Hymns, and
Spiritual Songs. Eph. v. 19.

Printed for the EDITOR, 1776.

The title page of George Thomson's Original Sacred Hymns

The sweet experience in divine things, particularly in the knowledge and the love of Jesus ... happily runs through them ... They may well be expected, from the very nature of their several subjects, under the dew of heaven, to promote in general an increasing knowledge of the redeemer, an humbling sense of sin, purity of heart, diligence in the paths of righteousness, and all the fruits of the Spirit. Nor is it imagined, that there is a single hymn, in which any denomination of Christians, to whom Christ, his word, and grace are precious, cannot readily join, or from which they will not receive some spiritual pleasure and profit. So unbigotted and so unbiased has been this child of light.[36]

The work was not easy at St Gennys for Thomson and occasionally he felt discouraged by the lack of progress. Once he was so downcast that he thought of quitting the parish for a better living elsewhere. Oblivious to the work God had done in many lives, he announced to his congregation that after thirty years' labour at the church he had not seen a single person converted through his ministry; he therefore intended to leave. After the service a woman hurried into the vestry and told him how she had been awakened under his teaching, and many others also testified to the help they had received. After welcoming the good news and thanking God for his grace, he decided to continue at St Gennys. As late as 1823, forty-one years after his death, a traveller on his way through Devon and Cornwall discovered that Thomson's memory was still honoured around St Gennys. He found 'several real worthies' and heard of 'many others', who were probably living converts of their late vicar. 'He laboured for many years in this parish,' notes the writer, 'as he thought in vain, but his work is with the Lord.'[37]

By 1765 he had stopped itinerating in order to concentrate on his own parish, holding services twice on Sundays, 'save in the dead quarter'. The average number of communicants had dropped from seventy to fifty, but he continued his summer and Lent catechising. Six years later the population of the parish had decreased to about fifty families. He continued to preach twice on a Sunday in the summer, but only once in the winter, and as before celebrated the Lord's Supper five times a year and catechised the young people. By now there were 'many dissenters' in the parish, though they had no meeting house. In 1779, in line with the falling population, his communicants numbered only forty. The decline at St Gennys was reflected throughout the Anglican Church. It was only after many 'enlightened' clergy were raised up that numbers started to increase.

In 1776, when Thomson was seventy-eight, Samuel Furly observed that the vigour of his mind was entirely unabated so that 'you hear, with astonishment, the amazing liveliness of youth'. His conversation was easy and vivacious, making it 'agreeable and amiable to a degree incredible', and the 'sallies of imagination' that sprang from him gave 'so much innocent delight, and yield[ed] so much instruction to his friends'.[38]

Throughout many discouragements Thomson persevered and faithfully conducted his ministry. He was now over eighty and practically blind. Seymour thinks he was blind for several years before his death, but he certainly signed the register, though with a tremulous hand, up to 26 November 1781. Although there was a very steep ascent from the vicarage to the church— Arthur Mee states that the 'churchyard is so steep that one of its paths is almost level with the roof'[39]—making it very difficult for a man of his age to climb, he refused to reduce his workload. Only for the last six months of his life did he employ a Mr Williams as curate.

In August 1782 Thomson was at the point of death. John Wesley, who had first preached for Thomson thirty-seven years before, heard that he was seriously ill while he was preaching in the street at Camelford and that his old friend wanted to see him. Although he was seventy-nine years old, he quickly borrowed the best horse he could find and set out on 3 September. He rode as fast as he could and arrived to a cold reception from Thomson's family. 'I found Mr Thompson just alive, but quite sensible. It seemed to me,' remarked Wesley, 'as if none in the house but himself was very glad to see me.' Thomson was very weak but conscious, and apprehensive about his approaching death, his mind filled with doubts and disquiet about his final state. Wesley said that he 'rather feared than desired to die'. The great preacher managed to 'comfort

John Wesley

him, and to increase and confirm his confidence in God'. He then asked if he could take Holy Communion, which Wesley administered to them both, the others refusing to partake. Afterwards Wesley, who left with mixed feelings, commented, 'I left him much happier than I found him, calmly waiting till his change should come.'[40] Within a few weeks, on 12 November 1782, Thomson was called home to receive the reward of the righteous. He was buried in the family vault at Barnstaple.

Thomson was a man of average height, and his voice had a pleasant trace of the Devonshire dialect. Like his father, he had a strong love of music and his mind was strongly emotional. He possessed an attractive and cheerful personality, delightful manners, and was apt to be jocular, much to the enjoyment of the company he kept. He was a writer of considerable ability—James Hervey testified that he had 'the most brilliant style of any man I know'—with a good poetical turn. He was a man of lively passions, fervent in his friendships, bold and zealous in his declarations of the gospel. Davidson, who corresponded with him, calls him a Christian of 'excellent temper and humble spirit'.[41] Furly paints this glowing portrait of Thomson:

No one, I believe, having ever yet the most sight or superficial acquaintance with this worthy, venerable man, but their admiration was excited, and their love raised ...

A clergyman, who has been intimate with him for several years, has often spoken, with the greatest admiration of the exalted height, and the uncommon extensiveness of this signal Christian grace [of love] in this truly eminent man, who breathes so much the spirit of benevolence in his words and actions, as would seem almost incredible to those, who through the workings of natural pride, worldliness and selfishness, are but of low attainments in grace and in the divine life ...

[Furly refers to Thomson's] steady zeal, singular faithfulness, his extraordinary love, and his benign friendliness. Every discerning eye can perceive that he really entertains mean thoughts of himself. With that humility that arises from a sense of great sinfulness *in the sight* of God and consequent unworthiness ... he casts his soul daily at the foot of Jesus' cross, looking wholly unto *mere* mercy ... In the gifts of nature, as well as in some others of grace, he stands particularly distinguished.[42]

In his preaching he was forceful and dramatic, and in many respects similar to Whitefield, endeavouring, by all possible means, to awaken, call and invite sinners to accept, with broken and penitent hearts, the gospel of Christ. It is not known to any but God what success he enjoyed, although Davidson points to 'the conversion of numbers in his parish'. While it is true that Thomson was more a son of consolation than a son of thunder, there was one occasion when his preaching had the 'surprising effect of lightning'.

A young gentleman in the ministry ... went to hear him ... when, to the astonishment of the audience ... as he was listening attentively to the discourse, he suddenly fell to the ground prostrate on his face; and unhappily rose with the entire loss of his senses. Near a twelve month he continued in that extremely pitiful and distressed condition. During which time continual prayers were offered up with peculiar fervour for his deliverance, the restoration of his reason, and the blessing of the almighty upon his soul. At last, God ... not only [gradually] restored to the young gentleman his reason, but together with that blessing vouchsafed also the inestimable gift of faith in Jesus with all its attendant graces ... Since which the pious youth, *now* grown more in years, has continued a faithful, conscientious, useful minister of Christ; powerfully bearing witness to that *grace*, of which he is himself so remarkable an instance.[43]

Three hymns in Thomson's *Sacred Hymns* were occasioned by this extraordinary event.

He was also extremely generous, which led to another astonishing incident. It was his custom for many years, after having supplied his own household, to distribute the surplus of his farm among his poor parishioners. He acted on a favourite maxim: 'it is enough for the present grass to feed its lamb'; so he took the produce of his 'little glebe' (approximately 27 acres) and divided it among the farmless inhabitants of the village. One year he promised to subscribe £30 towards the expense of building a chapel in a distant town, where the parishioners were too numerous to be well accommodated in their own parish church. However, he was unable to raise the money any other way than by selling some of the harvest usually reserved for his own poor parishioners, an expedient that 'became very painful to his feelings'.

Having collected the £30, he left home on his horse to deliver the money himself. On his journey he overtook a young lady to whom he said cheerfully, 'Well overtaken, fair lady. Will you accept of an old clergyman for your companion over the down? I am too old, indeed, to promise you much protection; but I trust God will protect both.' She was glad of his company and, as they soon discovered they were travelling to the same town, they rode on together. Thomson made the most of the opportunity, and with simplicity and godly sincerity that could not offend, shared with her the gospel. He also mentioned his name and the name of his church, and how dear his poor parishioners were to him, but he purposely did not refer to his generosity towards them. When they arrived at the town and were about to part, Thomson told his travelling companion the name of the friend to whose house he was going, and invited her to call on them.

That evening, in the course of conversation with her friends, she told them about the 'very agreeable old clergyman' she met on the road, whose name was Thomson, and about the many interesting subjects they had discussed. 'Thomson!' cried the lady of the house. 'I wish it was the Thomson we have been so many years inquiring after in vain. I have £30 tied up in a bag by my late husband, due to a person of that name, who desired to leave it till called for. But I suppose that he is dead; and his executor, whoever he be, knows nothing of it.' 'Who can tell,' answered the young lady, 'whether Mr Thomson may not know if it should have been any relation of his? Suppose we send to beg him to call here.'

The lady of the house agreed, and sent a servant to ask Thomson to visit them. Thomson immediately complied. He was told the reason why they had sent for him, from which it transpired that the Captain Thomson in the East India Service to whom this money had been so long due, was none other than his own brother, who had been dead for several years and for whom he was the executor and residuary legatee. When the lady of the house gave him the bag with the £30 in it, he could not stop himself from loudly expressing his thanks to God and pouring out deep affection for his poor parishioners. In front of them all, he fell on his knees, and with his eyes lifted up, he exclaimed, 'Blessed be God! How gracious, how wonderful, thus to provide for my poor people at home! The money will be theirs again.' He hurried back to tell his friend what had happened. As soon as he entered the house, he cried out, 'Praise God: tell it in Gath, publish it in Askelon, that our God is a faithful God!'[44]

G.C.B. Davies rightly comments that Thomson, along with Bennet and John Turner of Week St Mary, was one of the pioneers of Cornish evangelicalism. 'Despite considerable hostility from their brother clergy, the general apathy of the times, and low moral standards, they pursued their ministries in an earnest endeavour by any means to win the souls of their flocks.'[45] Although Thomson had a low opinion of his own labours, many ordinary lives were transformed through his preaching, and several less prominent evangelical clergy in Cornwall benefited from his encouragement and leadership. He was an evangelical pioneer, who must not be forgotten.

Endnotes

1 **George Thomson,** *Original Sacred Hymns* (Samuel Furly, 1776), pp. ii–iii.

2 *Ibid.*, pp. iii–iv.

3 *Christian Observer*, 1877, p. 65.

4 *Evangelical Magazine*, June 1800, p. 222.

5 *Ibid.*, p. 223.

6 **Thomson,** *Original Sacred Hymns*, p. v.

7 **Thomas Gibbons,** *Memoirs of Isaac Watts* (London, 1780), pp. 433–434.

8 *Christian Observer*, 1877, p. 62.

9 **Luke Tyerman,** *The Oxford Methodists* (London, Hodder & Stoughton, 1873), p. 229.

10 Miss R. had a younger sister, Miss C., who is also mentioned in Hervey's letters. According to Lysons, the 'heiress of the Thomsons married the Rev. S. May, in whose family the Devonshire property descended'. (*Christian Observer*, 1877, p. 65).

11 **Tyerman,** *Oxford Methodists*, pp. 242–244.

12 **George M. Ella,** *James Hervey: Preacher of Righteousness* (Eggleston, Go Publications, 1977), pp. 65–66.

13 *Christian Observer*, 1877, p. 61.

14 **Luke Tyerman,** *The Life of George Whitefield* (London, Hodder & Stoughton, 1876), vol. 1, p. 184.

15 *Ibid.*, vol. 2, p. 78.

16 **Charles Wesley,** *The Journal of Charles Wesley* (Grand Rapids, Baker Book House, 1908 reprint), vol. 1, p. 369.

17 **Tyerman,** *Whitefield*, vol. 2, p. 79.

18 Luke Tyerman, *The Life and Times of John Wesley* (London, Hodder & Stoughton, 1890), vol. 1, p. 458.

19 John Rowe, *Cornwall in the Age of the Industrial Revolution* (St Austell, Cornish Hillside Publications, 1993 reprint), p. 67.12, n. 12.

20 John Wesley, *The Works of John Wesley* (Grand Rapids, Baker Book House, 1998 reprint), vol. 1, p. 498.

21 *Ibid.,* vol. 2, p. 116.

22 Philip Doddridge, *The Life of Colonel James Gardiner* (Halifax, W. Milner, 1844), p. 40.

23 *Evangelical Magazine*, June 1800, p. 223.

24 *Ibid.,* p. 224.

25 *Ibid.*

26 G.R. Balleine, *A History of the Evangelical Party in the Church of England* (London, Longmans, Green & Co., 1909), p. 97.

27 *Christian Observer*, 1877, p. 63.

28 Wesley, *Works*, vol. 2, p. 205.

29 Tyerman, *Whitefield*, vol. 2, p. 253.

30 *Ibid.,* p. 254.

31 Wesley, *Works*, vol. 2, p. 300.

32 *Christian Observer*, 1877, p. 64.

33 Thomson, *Original Sacred Hymns*, pp. 106–107.

34 *Ibid.,* p. 204.

35 *Ibid.,* p. ix.

36 *Ibid.,* p. xi.

37 By an Old Traveller, *A Narrative of a Tour in the West of England* (London, John Offor, 1823), p. 33.

38 Thomson, *Original Sacred Hymns*, pp. viii, ix.

39 Athur Mee (editor), *Cornwall* (London, Hodder & Stoughton, 1951 reprint), p. 216.

40 Wesley, *Works*, vol. 4, p. 235.

41 *Evangelical Magazine*, June 1800, p. 225.

42 Thomson, *Original Sacred Hymns*, pp. i, vii–viii.

43 *Ibid.,* pp. xii–xiii.

44 *Zion's Trumpet, a Theological Miscellany* (Bristol, 1799), pp. 449–452.

45 G.C.B. Davies, *The Early Cornish Evangelicals 1735–60* (London, SPCK, 1951), p. 50.

James Rouquet

The poor man's preacher

James Rouquet was born in 1730, the son of Huguenot refugees. According to Caleb Evans, a Baptist minister in Bristol, his grandfather was 'condemned to the galleys on account of his religion. He endured the greatest hardships for many years but was at length delivered by the unexpected interposition of a stranger', which fulfilled a 'remarkable dream of that happy event, which the old gentleman had just before'.[1] His father, Anthony Rouquet, a French Protestant refugee, 'for the sake of his life, liberty and religion was constrained to leave his native country, and to abandon those fair prospects of wealth and comparative greatness to which he was born'.[2]

Little is known about Rouquet's early years except that he was a 'sprightly genius', whose abilities soon opened the way into one of the most celebrated public schools in London, the Merchant Taylors' School off Cannon Street. From nine to seventeen he was educated there in the various branches of classical learning. During the course of his studies he was led providentially to hear the great preacher George Whitefield and other ministers, and by the grace of God was called effectually to a saving knowledge of Christ in his early youth. 'His convictions were lasting, and remarkably deep and pungent; so that for a considerable time together his only cry by night and by day was, with a distress bordering on distraction, "What must I do to be saved?" At length, the terrors of the law were subdued by the grace of the gospel, and he had that peace in believing, which passeth all understanding.'[3]

On 16 July 1748, at eighteen years of age, he matriculated at St John's College, Oxford, where he stayed, according to Caleb Evans, 'three years, during which time, his piety and holy zeal were no less conspicuous than his steadiness and diligence in attending to the college exercises'.[4] However, the St John's records inform us that his caution money (a sum deposited as security for good behaviour) was returned in December 1749, suggesting that he never claimed his degree.

James Rouquet

The first Kingswood school in Bristol, built by John Wesley and George Whitefield

Four days after Rouquet matriculated, Charles Wesley, who had been showing Sally Gwynne, whom he married on 8 April 1749, round the Oxford colleges, wrote in his *Journal* that he 'met a poor servitor of St John's, James Rouquet, who is not ashamed to confess Christ before men'.[5] While at college he received 'repeated and pressing invitations' to preside over John Wesley's boarding school at Kingswood. Finally in mid-term, probably in 1751, he accepted 'upon the purest motives'. Evans says that during the three or four years he spent at the school, he 'acquitted himself with singular success' and 'preached frequently as opportunity occurred'.[6]

Wesley hoped that the school would not only teach its pupils knowledge and godliness, but that it would be an Academy for the training of young itinerant preachers. He planned to take about fifty boys, who would be taught by a 'group of his trusted lieutenants, six of them, semi-itinerant preachers, young men of scholarship and integrity'.[7] Within two or three months of its opening, twenty-eight boys, sons of the friends of Wesley's connexion, were attending the school. At first all went well. The housekeeper wrote that the 'spirit of this family is a resemblance of the household above';[8] and early in 1749, when there were twenty-one boarders and twelve preachers in training, John's 'sons in the gospel', Charles Wesley wrote in his *Journal* that he thought his brother was 'laying the foundation of many generations'.

However, it was not long before problems arose. The Wesleys, often away for long periods, did not appoint a headmaster to run the school, and so the discipline and organization of the students were not monitored as closely as they would have liked. 'The quality and quantity of religious practice and emotion … expected from young boys was ill-judged,' and the marriages of four principal men, one of them to the housekeeper, was unsettling. When John returned from Ireland in 1749, he discovered that 'several of the rules had been habitually neglected' and that it was 'necessary to lessen the family; suffering none to remain therein, who were not clearly satisfied with them, and determined to observe them all'.[9] By September 1750, four of the masters and the housekeeper had left, with the other two leaving not long afterwards.

It was into this unstable situation that Rouquet arrived in an effort to re-establish the school. At the end of the following year he advertised the school in *Felix Farley's Bristol Journal*, detailing the broad curriculum, with the comment that 'particular care is also taken of the morals of the children, that they be trained at once to learning and virtue'.[10] There is no mention of religious exercises or of Wesley's 'famous rules', such as no child should be out of the sight of a master.

Evidently Kingswood made a fresh start under Rouquet, who to begin with was given a free hand. His only assistant was John Maddern, who married Molly Francis, the headmistress of the parallel girls' school. However, in August 1753, when Wesley inspected the school, he was still not happy. 'I endeavoured once more to bring Kingswood School into order. Surely the importance of this design is apparent, even from the difficulties that attend it. I have spent more money, and time, and care, on this, than almost any design I ever had. And still it exercises all the patience I have. But it is worth all the labour.'[11] Years later, on 2 January 1769, Wesley wrote to Joseph Benson, who had become the headmaster the previous year, and commented, 'Rouquet, John Jones [Rouquet's predecessor] and Mr [Walter] Sellon were far better scholars than Mr [John] Parkinson,' who had succeeded Rouquet and died at the school.

It is not certain exactly when Rouquet left Kingswood, but soon after his departure he applied for orders in the Church of England, hoping he might become more useful in the kingdom of God. On 22 September 1754 he was ordained deacon by the Bishop of Gloucester, Dr Johnston, and willingly subscribed to the thirty-nine Articles. He was licensed to serve the cure of Sandhurst in the diocese of Gloucester, but, as Caleb Evans states, his 'fidelity and zeal were ... too great to admit of his long continuance in the curacy ... and he was therefore soon dismissed from it'.[12] He obviously found it difficult to settle into the restrictions of a parish, but he felt compelled to

Lady Huntingdon. Rouquet was
'one of her most valued and
intimate friends'

preach the gospel, and the following year Wesley, alluding to his 'Methodist instincts', listed him among his half-itinerants.

It was probably in the summer of 1754, when Wesley was recuperating at the Hot Wells in Bristol, that Rouquet first met Lady Huntingdon. According to Seymour, after a shaky start to the relationship, he became 'one of her most valued and intimate friends'.[13] The countess spoke of Rouquet's engagement to Sarah Fenwicke, the sister of the Countess of Deloraine and daughter of Edward Fenwicke of Charles Town, South Carolina, in three letters to Charles Wesley. In the first (October 1754), she expressed her shock at the rumoured affair and asks, 'Who is the man—what is he?' Rouquet, in her eyes, was just a 'commoner'. A year later she mentioned 'poor Rouquet's approaches to Miss Fenwicke', and in January 1756 she wrote that she could not 'remember anything being said of Mr Rouquet's beliefs or enthusiasm or his several courtships', although she had spoken with him about his 'unsettled disposition and irregularity', and on that account was not ready to write to the archbishop about his ordination.[14]

Rouquet's courtship with Sarah Fenwicke began towards the end of 1754, and two years later, in September 1756, they were married at St Luke's, Old Street, London. Sarah is registered a spinster of St George's, Hanover Square, where William Romaine had been appointed assistant morning preacher in 1750. Romaine's ministry there lasted five years. The marriage certificate was signed by two witnesses: John Wesley and A. Rouquet. The following year the Earl of Deloraine appointed Rouquet to be one of his domestic chaplains. The Rouquets had six children, three of whom survived James. Sarah, who is described as an 'amiable and pious lady', died on 28 April 1768. Five years later, on 13 March 1773, James married Mary, the widow of John Cannon of Greenwich, 'with whom he lived in a state of the most perfect conjugal felicity to the time of his death'.[15]

After his ordination in 1754 Rouquet devoted his time to preaching the gospel in Bristol, making the most of every opportunity. 'A happy necessity was laid upon him,' says Caleb Evans, 'and he could as soon have ceased to be, as ceased to be active in his master's work, ceased to preach the everlasting gospel, which he had felt in his own soul was the power of God to salvation. Accordingly he not only preached from house to house, but to crowded auditories in the common prison of the city, and it pleased God remarkably to bless his labours to many.'[16] His work in Bristol prison became very important to him, and he treasured the occasions presented to him. Rowland Hill says, 'Though the inhabitants of gaols are generally accounted the dung and off scouring of all things, yet without the least expectation of any earthly advantage, it is known to all, he was their constant friend. *As a minister*, his labours of love for the good of their souls were ever at their service. *As a man*, he esteemed it his happiness to promote their advantage and redeem them from misery, as if their cases were his own.'[17]

On 24 August 1755, according to a notice in *Felix Farley's Bristol Journal* for the preceding day, Rouquet preached at Newgate Prison at eight in the morning. He preached there again the next week and at Bedminster in September. On 28 September he preached a 'condemned sermon' in the morning and another at four in the afternoon 'to the prisoner Williams now under sentence of death in Newgate who will be executed on Friday next'. He had probably already been appointed chaplain or ordinary to Newgate. His ministry in prisons lasted until the day of his death.

During this time Rouquet's relationship with John Wesley was developing. He attended his conference in 1755, and bravely attempted to fill the dual role of clergyman and Methodist. However, he seems to have had some difficulties with Mrs Wesley, for John wrote to his wife from Liverpool on 22 April 1757 and said, 'I am afraid Jemmy Rouquet's head is not quite right: I have written him a long, mild, loving answer.'[18] The following year, Wesley wrote to Elizabeth Hardy and, in referring to their views of perfection, coupled Rouquet with Thomas Walsh, of whom he thought so highly. 'You yourself believed twenty years ago that we should not put off the infection of nature but with our bodies. I did so. But I believe otherwise now for many reasons ... How far Mr Rouquet or Mr Walsh may have mistaken these I know not.'[19]

Rouquet preached at Newgate Prison again in April 1759 and a collection was taken for needy prisoners, who returned 'hearty thanks' to him for 'unwearied diligence' and for being 'instrumental in procuring them the blessing of liberty'. In true humility he wrote in the *Bristol Journal* that their

... thanks are rather due to the gentlemen and ladies who upon my mentioning their distress, so generously contributed to their enlargement. An example well worthy of imitation of their fellow citizens; while some who might be useful members of society are yet languishing in a miserable confinement likely to be rendered more so by the severities of the approaching season. And indeed the late instance of humanity towards our enemies the late French prisoners at Knowle, encourages us to hope that friends and fellow subjects will not be suffered to pine in misery and want at the very time when God (not weighing our merits, for we are a rebellious house) has mercifully turned our days of fasting and mourning into days of thanksgiving and joy, by the late miraculous successes [in the Seven Years' War] of this ever memorable year—ought you not to have compassion on your fellow servant even as I had on you?[20]

The reference to 'French prisoners at Knowle' was because Wesley had earlier called on the humanity and generosity of Bristol to clothe the poor naked prisoners, who were held there.

Rouquet continued his charitable work at the prison and supplied many of the needs of the inmates. When Wesley returned to Newgate, he was amazed at the change for good that had taken place. On 2 January 1761 he wrote to the editor of the *London Chronicle* with the good news.

Of all the seats of woe on this side of hell, few, I suppose, exceed or even equal Newgate. If any region of horror could exceed it a few years ago, Newgate in Bristol did; so great was the filth, the stench, the misery and wickedness, which shocked all who had a spark of humanity left. How was I surprised then, when I was there a few weeks ago! 1. Every part of it, above stairs and below, even the pit, wherein the felons are confined at night, is as clean and sweet as a gentleman's house; it being now a rule, that every prisoner wash and clean his apartment thoroughly twice a week. 2. Here is no fighting or brawling ... 3. The usual grounds for quarrelling are removed. For it is very rarely that any one cheats or wrongs another ... 4. Here is no drunkenness suffered

... 5. Nor any whoredom; the women prisoners being narrowly observed, and kept separate from the men ... 6. All possible care is taken to prevent idleness. Those who are willing to work at their callings are provided with tools and materials ... 7. Only on the Lord's Day they neither work nor play, but dress themselves as clean as they can to attend the public service in the chapel, at which every person under the roof is present ... 8. And in order to assist them in things of the greatest concern (besides a sermon every Sunday and Thursday), they have a large Bible chained on one side of the chapel, which any of the prisoners may read. By the blessing of God on these regulations, the prison now has a new face. Nothing offends the eye or ear, and the whole has the appearance of a quiet, serious family.[21]

The change for the better in prison conditions must be attributed, at least in part, to the efforts of Rouquet.

In 1759 Rouquet was no doubt delighted with the appointment to St George's of the evangelical vicar, Richard Hart. Hart had been educated at Christ Church, Oxford, before becoming curate of Warminster, where he was converted under the ministry of Joseph Williams of Kidderminster. When he moved to St George's, it was a real spiritual boost for Bristol. He was a friendly man of great zeal for the gospel, and was one of the only two men who replied by letter to Wesley's appeal for unity in 1764.

James Brown, who may have been Rouquet's contemporary at Oxford, was another of the 'enlightened' Bristol clergy. In 1756 Brown was curate of Bradford, where he embraced the gospel, again under the ministry of Williams. He became under-master of Bristol Grammar School, and in 1759, minor canon of the Cathedral. He left Bristol two years later to become the vicar of West Harptree in Somerset and was succeeded there by Rouquet in 1765. He was one of three rectors who signed Rouquet's testimonial and both men preached at the anniversary of Trevecca College. Seymour calls

Trevecca College, where Rouquet preached an anniversary sermon

Edward Colston, a popular benefactor of Bristol, providing money for various charities throughout his life

him 'an elegant scholar, and a warm-hearted and generous friend. His sentiments were refined by the sincerest piety, and his conversation was replete with true politeness, diversified and interesting.'[22] Lady Huntingdon thought him, in many respects, 'an extraordinary man. His classical knowledge, I am told, exceeds that of most men of his age and standing. His information is extensive, accurate and correct. His knowledge diversified and profound. But what I admire most is his zeal and devotedness of heart to God. His preaching is much admired, and is owned by the great Master of assemblies.'[23]

In March 1760, Rouquet was unanimously elected chaplain of the hospital on St Michael's Hill, which had been founded by Edward Colston, a pious and charitable man. In this capacity Rouquet further enhanced his reputation as a public figure in Bristol, so that even his domestic affairs were reported in the press. 'Last week,' wrote one paper in 1760, 'a servant of Rev. Mr Rouquet going down stone steps into the kitchen with a young child in her arms had the misfortune to fall, whereby the maid was greatly hurt and the child's head so desperately fractured that it is since dead.'[24]

On 30 March 1761, Wesley wrote to Rouquet and opened his heart about problems he was experiencing with his wife. There were only three or four men with whom Wesley shared such intimate domestic confidences, and it is further proof that he regarded Rouquet as a trusted friend.

Mrs John Wesley, about whom John wrote to Rouquet

Finding all other means ineffectual, on Monday ... I opened my wife's bureau and took what I found of my own ... Some hours after, she talked like an Empress Queen; on which I told her plainly, 'While you are in this mind I will neither bed nor board with you.' ... [Later] I found her of a better mind; so ... we were together as usual. But if we should live to meet again, and she behaves as she did on that day, I should think it my bounden duty to do as I did then. I judge her case to be proper lunacy; but it is a preternatural, a diabolical lunacy, and therefore *at those times* (I know what I say) I do not think my life is safe with her.[25]

John Wesley. Rouquet was one of the preacher's great friends

Previous to the above letter, when Wesley was having difficulties with his only ordained preacher Thomas Maxfield, Rouquet had written to him, expressing his desire for greater unity among the clergy. This in turn led Wesley to consider appealing again for a general union. In reply, he said,

The thing you mention has been much in my thoughts ... The dreadful consequences which have arisen from the disunion of Christian ministers, especially those whom God has lately employed, are too glaring to be hid from any who do not wilfully shut their eyes. How often has this put a sword into the hand of the common enemy! ... On the other hand, how many and how great are the advantages which would flow from a general *union*, of those at least who acknowledge each other to be messengers of God! I know nothing (but sin) which I would not do or leave undone to promote it; and this has been my settled determination for at least ten years last past. But all my overtures have been constantly rejected; almost all of them stand aloof and at length they have carried their point. I let them alone ...

However, if you can think of any expedient which is likely to avail, I will make a fresh trial.[26]

Wesley made a 'fresh trial' three years later in 1764, after Maxfield had left, when he called a conference of friendly Bristol clergy and then wrote to all the clergy throughout the country appealing for unity and help. Rouquet, of course, was included in the letter and almost certainly took part in the conference.

Two and a half months after Wesley's letter to Rouquet, in June 1761, *Felix Farley's Journal* noted the execution on St Michael's Hill of William Dillon Sheppard, who had been convicted of sodomy. On the day of his death he appeared penitent and behaved with 'surprising composure'. A few minutes before his execution he protested his innocence to the spectators. 'He was attended by the Rev. Mr Rouquet, who made an excellent and pathetic discourse on the occasion; and Tuesday afternoon preached a funeral sermon over his dead body in Newgate, from which he was carried and buried in a decent manner.'[27] Once again Rouquet made the most of the opportunity to preach the gospel.

In 1763, at the height of Wesley's problems with Thomas Maxfield, Rouquet wrote to his friend and expressed sympathy for the doctrines of Arminianism and perfectionism that he was propagating.

The word is, only believe! ... Jesus help my unbelief! This is all I wait to prove. O that I might see aright and never rest till I also have apprehended ... I would be the Lord's free-man. I would be all faith; all love I think I would. And yet were this my one desire, I believe the Lord would soon come to my help. I find that the converse of Christian friends is a great blessing. I am glad of the opportunities I enjoy, and I believe our meeting will be more profitable than ever, as our friend Mr Stonehouse has freely engaged me in a dispute (by writing) concerning perfection. To me it is the one thing needful. Therefore I cannot avoid being explicit on this head, in these meetings ... and to the Sunday morning congregation; and I feel an unspeakable blessing in so doing, as also in pressing the present now ... Above all I lament that any professing the renewal should be found so wanting in the main branches of it ... For my own part I freely own, I stand in doubt of every man whose meek and lowly walk does not prove that he has learned of Jesus ... Everyone that is perfect shall be as his Master.[28]

Not surprisingly Wesley later published this letter in the *Arminian Magazine*. As Rouquet increasingly associated with Calvinists, and in a reaction against Wesley's attacks on the doctrines of grace, he gradually embraced evangelicalism more fully.

On 8 July 1765 Rouquet was presented to the living of West Harptree by the Lord Chancellor, acting for Roy George the third, patron. West Harptree was a village on the Bristol side of the Mendips, where he stayed until his wife Sarah died. He was sponsored by James Brown and Lady Huntingdon, and instituted there by Edward Wills, Bishop of Bath and Wells. His friend Caleb Evans said, 'His Lordship, finding him to be a truly worthy man, notwithstanding the cry of Enthusiast! Methodist! which had been raised against him, received him with paternal affection, and spoke of him to many, in terms of the highest respect, to his dying day.'[29]

After his ordination Rouquet preached a 'most excellent sermon' from the words, 'Feed my sheep'. However, it offended many who heard it. On hearing about the uproar it caused, the bishop asked Rouquet for a copy of the sermon, which was immediately sent. While the bishop was considering his response, Peter Grigg of Ubley, whom Rouquet had been helping as curate for some time, and who had signed Rouquet's testimonial (the other signatories were James Brown, the outgoing rector, and Daniel Debat of Christ Church, Bristol), wrote to the bishop. 'He appears a good man,' said Grigg, 'and to have the welfare of mankind at heart. Since he has served my parish at Ubley, he has done it regularly and faithfully, endeavouring both by public preaching and private exhortations to make the people understand and practise their duty to God [and] to one another. Some I know, have been much benefited and reformed thereby and I hope nothing will prevent his more extensive usefulness in the place.'[30] When the bishop returned the sermon to Rouquet, he enclosed 'a most affectionate letter, expressing his entire approbation of it, and assuring him of the continuance of his friendship'.[31]

In the same year that Rouquet went to West Harptree, Captain Thomas Webb, who had lost an eye to musket-fire in 1759 while fighting at Montmorency in Canada, was converted after hearing Mr Cary, a Moravian minister, on Passion Sunday. The Moravian preacher introduced him to Rouquet, who in turn brought him among the Bristol Methodists, where he made his spiritual home. He enjoyed a 'fit so fine' among his new friends that he always regarded them and him as made for each other. He

Captain Thomas Webb, who has been called 'American Methodists' number one layman'

became a tireless worker on behalf of any Methodist concern in Britain and abroad, and was instrumental in securing funds for a second Methodist chapel in Bristol on Portland Heights, where on Christmas Eve 1796 he was buried.

From about 1766 Rouquet acted as Richard Symes's curate at St Werburgh's, a central church in the poorer part of the city, and was appointed by the Corporation 'lecturer' or preacher at St Nicholas. The next year he was unanimously chosen as chaplain of St Peter's Hospital, again following in the footsteps of James Brown. At this point, Caleb Evans remarks, 'The strict attention he paid to the duty of his several offices, and his incessant labours of love in private, particularly amongst the poor and distressed, to whom his benevolence was unbounded, are too well known to the whole city to need any further confirmation.'[32]

During that year he preached a charitable sermon at St Stephen's Church and afterwards at a dinner in the assembly room in Prince's Street, where the mayor, two sheriffs, and the members of parliament for Hereford and Gloucester were present, and £94 was collected for apprenticing poor boys. With these various appointments and engagements, it is not surprising that his great friend Rowland Hill, who preached his first sermon after ordination to a crowded congregation at St Werburgh's, said that he 'for many years of his life seldom used to preach less than seven times in the week ... He was one that never wished for higher

Rowland Hill, Rouquet's close friend

promotion than to dedicate his time, talents and all to the temporal and eternal good of the poor.'[33]

In January 1768 Rouquet gave a detailed account to the public of the monies received by him from December 1766 to December 1767 for the relief of prisons in Newgate. His intention was to encourage those who had already contributed and to stir up others to help the poor and oppressed objects of the charity. He also mentioned that of all the prisoners who had been released by his contributions, only one had been imprisoned a second time. He then pleaded on the prisoners' behalf, stressing their extreme poverty, the severity of the winter season, and above all the excessively high price of provisions, and promising that whatever monies for their relief came through his hands, would be applied in the most effectual manner.

The list of items on which the money had been spent included wine for the sick, sugar, salt, butter, a coat and flannel, an attorney for Saunders, shoes, a bed, the discharge of thirteen named prisoners, and bread and wine for the sacrament. The total came to £43 18s 1d, the exact amount of monies received. Rouquet recommended that all donors enquire first of the keeper as to what kind of provisions were most wanted and the times when they would be most needed, so that the best use could be made of all contributions. It appears that Matthew Brickdale, who represented the city in parliament, supported Rouquet's efforts. He may have been instrumental in getting the city to recognize officially the value of Rouquet's work, for in December 1769 'the attention of the Chamber [of Commerce] was directed … to the devoted ministerial services rendered by the Rev. James Rouquet to prisoners in the gaol for nearly twenty years. It was determined that a gift of £20 would be sufficient compensation.'[34]

In 1768 Rouquet published his *Prayer in Commemoration of Bristol's Benefactors*, which was republished in 1881 by William George. George also reprinted Rouquet's sermon on *The Christian Strife*, which was preached before the 'Grateful Society' at the parish church of All Saints on Monday 14 November 1768.

In that year, Rouquet was invited to Lady Huntingdon's house in Bath, and John Wesley, who was thought to be dying, made a will in which he left all his manuscripts to Rouquet, evidence, according to Sackett, of the 'high esteem and absolute confidence' he had in Rouquet's 'industry, scholarship and compatibility'.[35] Later in the year Wesley complimented his friend by associating him in scholarship with Dr Stonehouse. In a letter from Shoreham on 22 December to Joseph Benson, he said,

When I recommend to any one a method or scheme of study, I do not barely consider this or that book separately, but in conjunction with the rest. And what I recommend I know; I know both the style and sentiments of each author; and how he will confirm or illustrate what goes before, and prepare for what comes after. Now, supposing Mr Stonehouse, Ro[u]quet, or any other, to have ever so great learning and judgment, yet he does not enter into my plan. He does not comprehend my views, nor keep his eye fixed on the same point.[36]

In 1769 Lady Huntingdon, along with Whitefield and Wesley, visited Kingswood School. The following morning a group of local clergy, which almost certainly included Rouquet and James Brown, enjoyed breakfast with the countess at her house, and afterwards Wesley preached. In 1770 Rouquet joined Wesley in administering the sacrament in Bristol, and Wesley preached in St Werburgh's at least twice. Rouquet's connections with men such as Whitefield and Wesley show how involved he was with some of the principal leaders of the revival.

In 1769 Rouquet gave up the vicarage of West Harptree to D.S. Haynes, curate of St Werburgh's, Bristol, with whom he exchanged livings. He took the oath before he was licensed on 27 December 1770. Evans says that so 'attached was he to the poor prisoners, and the other distressed objects in [Bristol], to whom the Lord rendered him eminently useful, that no consideration could prevail upon him to remove hence', which is why he left West Harptree for the curacy of St Werburgh's, where he worked until his death.[37]

From early 1770 many letters appeared in *Felix Farley's Bristol Journal* about St Peter's Hospital, some of which openly criticized the practices of the hospital. According to the correspondents the hospital smelt, sheets had been unchanged for three months, and pointed questions were asked about the 'putrid fever' (typhus) that had killed the last two masters. Rouquet, as chaplain of the hospital, was suspected of raising the alarm.

Consequently he received a 'torrent of abuse', particularly from Dr Rigge, who accused him of betraying the trust put in him. However, he was innocent of the charges and protested strongly against the unjust treatment he had received. He wrote to Rigge and said, 'You will be sorry at the unkind things ... said of me when I assure you ... I had no concern at all in any of the writings which have appeared ... save only, at the request of a friend, I did assist him in drawing up two papers signed C. P. which he did afterwards alter and correct to his own liking. There is the real truth.' To this protestation Rigge unsympathetically replied, 'You have at last cried *peccavi* [a confession of guilt] ... The plot begins to unravel and he and I may perhaps ... come to an *éclaircissement* [an explanation of the mystery].'[38] At least after this rebuff, the charges against Rouquet were dropped.

In 1771 Rouquet and James Brown served Lady Huntingdon's chapel in Bath while she was away, before the former was asked to preach at the opening of her Tabernacle at Trowbridge, an engagement that according to Seymour lasted for the rest of his life. 'Such was the liberality manifested by Mr Ro[u]quet towards the dissenters and Methodists, with whom in all essential points of doctrine he was one in heart and mind, that to the day of his death he continued to preach the anniversary sermon at Trowbridge, without any notice being taken of his irregularity.'[39] He also preached at the third anniversary of the founding of Trevecca before a distinguished gathering of ministers.

The following year Rouquet was involved in a controversy involving Jonathan Britain, a prisoner who was executed for forgery on St Michael's Hill gallows. On the day of his execution Britain 'behaved with remarkable decency and penitence and devotion, sung, prayed and exhorted the people with much fervour and affection, acknowledged the justice of his sentence, declared his hearty forgiveness of all his persecutors and was turned off about 2 o'clock expressing his pious hope of immortality'.[40] Soon afterwards it was alleged that Britain had withdrawn his confession before he died and a newspaper controversy followed.

In support of Britain, Rouquet wrote a preface to a pamphlet entitled *Some Particulars of the Life and Death of Jonathan Britain*—by a gentleman who attended him, published by William Pine, in which he testified, contrary to the pamphlet's insinuations, to the truth of Britain's repentance. It is a good example of Rouquet's ability to defend those who could not defend themselves.

His soul was contrite and his heart wounded within him. With strong cries and tears, and with a deep abhorrence of himself and sin, not easy to be expressed, he made supplication to his God; until God, ever mindful of his promise made to the returning sinner, answered him in the joy of his heart. His time was now short, but every hour of it was crowded with the most grateful returns for the mercy he had received ...

His works fully justified his faith, and bore witness for him, that he was born of God. He gave convincing proofs of the most humble ... resignation to the fate which he had so justly merited; and of that love and faith, and steady patience, with which it pleased God so mercifully to arm his breast ...

His prayers, and tears, and earnest monitory addresses to the surrounding multitude, in his way to execution, bespoke the solemn awe which rested on his soul; and also the praises, which he so affectionately poured forth to him that loved him, and washed him in his blood, gave comfortable testimony of a good hope through grace.

It is allowed, that public executions should be strikingly awful, and Britain always wished to maintain such a conduct as might contribute to make his so. How far he supported such a conduct let his solemn, earnest, repeated admonitions, at the fatal tree, to old and young; his pointing out to them the steps, by which he had brought himself to ruin; his affectionate and pressing invitations to them all to turn to God; his fervent addresses to heaven; the tears and prayers of the many thousands who attended the execution, together with that deep, expressive seriousness and awe, which sat on every face:—I say, let this testify.[41]

William Talbot, the vicar of St Giles', Reading, put in a good word for Rouquet in his *Narrative of the Whole of his Proceedings Relative to Jonathan Britain*. He said, 'Mr Rouquet is a gentleman of whose zeal in the cause of religion I have heard much spoken; and of whose disinterested attendance upon, and assiduity among, the criminals in Newgate I have heard great commendations.'[42] The controversy was finally ended by a letter written under a pseudonym, and printed and countersigned by Pine:

As the character of the Rev. Mr Rouquet has been much injured by the unjust and illiberal insinuation of being author [of the above pamphlet] ... I think it incumbent on me to make public declaration that he was in no way concerned therein ... And as several other pieces that lately made their appearance were unjustly ascribed to the pen of that gentleman, I assured myself the printer will join with me ... in the following act of public justice ... The narrative respecting Jonathan Britain ... was *not* the product of Mr Rouquet.[43]

Rouquet's relationship with John Wesley was tested when the latter published the *Minutes* of his 1772 conference, in which he made an undisguised attack on Calvinism and adopted an extreme Arminian position. This may well have contributed to pushing Rouquet in the opposite direction, for in the same year

The Foundery, where Rouquet preached a 'Calvinistic' sermon

Rouquet 'helped' Wesley in Bristol, and preached at the Foundery in London, where his sermon offended many. In reference to Rouquet, John Pawson wrote to Matthew Magor:

Rouquet ... is disaffected towards us. He has been in London for some time with his dear friend Mr [Rowland] Hill. One night he preached in the Foundery, where he gave universal offence by using many Calvinistical phrases, and by telling the whole congregation that he knew there were whores and bawds even in the Bands [Methodist meetings] in Bristol. He said, 'These eyes have seen it, and this heart has groaned on account of it.' How he will be when he returns I know not; but these are the accounts we hear from London. Were it not that so many of our people are so exceedingly unstable, we need not fear any of these things; but you well know that many of them have got itching ears, and will run about, say or do what we will.[44]

Wesley was quick to reprove his friend Rouquet, who wrote back to him with grace and no ill feeling. Wesley then wrote to his brother Charles (4 November), 'I have an *exceeding loving letter* from J.[ames] R.[ouquet], in answer to my plain one. So, if it did him no good (but possibly it might), at least it did him no harm. If we duly join faith and works in all our preaching, we shall not fail of a blessing.'[45] Rouquet's close relationship with two forthright Calvinists, Rowland Hill and Caleb Evans (Wesley's political opponent), and his adoption of their views, alienated him, not so much from Wesley, but from Wesley's followers, some of whom did not want to assign to Rouquet his rightful place in Methodist history. In 1801, in a letter from Pawson to Atmore, who was compiling *Memorials of the Methodist Preachers*, the former said, 'As to Mr Rouquet I think you had better let him alone as he never was a travelling preacher, his last days were not his best; his sun set under a cloud.' This deprecatory comment could only refer to Rouquet's Calvinism, which many found distasteful.

In January 1773 Rouquet published his own financial statement. The income for his charity work had increased to £136. In the summer he was in London and may have contacted the London Society, from whom his new scheme *The Bristol Society for Relief and Discharge of Persons Confined for Small Debts* originated. At the end of the year a letter of his was published, which links him with the similar movement in London:

For near twenty years I have officiated as a clergyman in the prison of Newgate and promoted the relief and discharge of prisoners to the utmost of my power amidst a variety of difficulties and discouragements. I have, however, the satisfaction to observe that of some hundreds of prisoners who have been set at liberty during that period not more than six or eight have been imprisoned a second time and that their enlargement has proved a real advantage to society as well as comfort to themselves. Encouraged by the generous assistance I have … received from the public support of the scheme, I wish to see it pursued in a more general and extensive form as near as may be like that of the Thatched House Society in London.[46]

He goes on to propose that all who support his scheme should meet on 12 January 1774 at the Fountain Tavern in High Street. By May it was reported that twenty-five persons had been discharged for £37 13s, and

nineteen wives and forty-eight children had
been released from deplorable situations.
Farley's Bristol Journal comments, 'The
feeling heart must at once discover the
great utility to society in general as well as
the humanity to poor distressed
individuals which the plan so evidently
tends to provide.'47

In September 1774 Rouquet, along with
the Wesleys, Caleb Evans, John Fletcher of
Madeley and others, became embroiled in a
controversy about American taxation. The
crux of the matter was that the American
colonists were aggrieved about being
taxed without their consent by the
English parliament. According to Evans,
John Wesley had recommended to

*John Fletcher of Madeley, who
became embroiled in a controversy
over American taxation*

William Pine that he print the pamphlet *An Argument in Defence of the
Exclusive Right Claimed by the Colonies to Tax Themselves*. The
following year, in a complete turn around, Wesley wrote to his brother
and accused Pine of printing 'bare-faced treason'. He urged Charles to
warn him, 'and if he slights or forgets this warning, then give him his
choice, either to leave us quietly, or to be publicly disowned'.48 He then
exhorted Pine to take care not to be 'carried away with the torrent. You
stand on slippery ground. I have written more largely to Mr Rouquet, and
refer you to his letter for particulars. Let no warm man persuade you to
take any step which you may repent as long as you live.'49

To back up his 'forgetfulness', Wesley, in the preface to the first edition of
his *Calm Address to our American Colonies* in which he defended the
English position, claimed he had never seen the pamphlet he had
supposedly recommended to Pine. Rouquet, who knew differently, wrote to
Wesley and reminded him that it was at his house that he had urged his
brother Charles to read it. Wesley wrote to Rouquet on 8 November 1775,
stating, 'I remember nothing of that book, neither of the title nor of the
argument. But I will send to the bookseller's tomorrow for the book; and if

I have read, I cannot but remember when I see it again.' Four days later he again wrote to Rouquet and made the following admission:

Dear James, I will now simply tell you the thing as it is. As I was returning from the Leeds Conference, one gave me the tract which you refer to, part of which I read on my journey. The spirit of it I observed to be admirably good; and I *then* thought the arguments conclusive [though he was to change his mind after reading Samuel Johnson's work]. In consequence of which, I suppose (though I do not remember it) I recommended it both to you and others; but I had so entirely forgotten it, that even when it was brought to me the other day, I could not recollect that I had seen it.[50]

On 25 November, Wesley wrote a long and controversial letter to *Farley's Journal*, in which he admitted taking much of his *Calm Address* from Samuel Johnson's *Taxation no Tyranny*. He again denied knowledge of the book he had recommended to Pine. Caleb Evans would have none of it, and declared that 'Rouquet, a worthy clergyman of the Church of England', would make an 'oath if required that John Wesley recommended the aforesaid book to him ... and to his brother Charles at his (Rouquet's) room'.[51] Wesley refused to admit he was wrong and wrote a long reply in his defence.

John Fletcher also got involved. He sent Wesley a manuscript entitled *A Second Check to Civil Antinomianism*, which was an extract from the Church of England Homily on Rebellion. He wanted Wesley to print and circulate it, not only for the general good, but 'to shame Ro[u]quet', who Fletcher thought had turned against his friend Wesley and sided with his opponent, Caleb Evans. Luke Tyerman comments, 'Wesley seems to have had more regard for Mr Ro[u]quet's reputation, than even gentle-minded Fletcher had, for Fletcher's manuscript was not published.'[52] This unsavoury controversy may explain why Caleb Evans and Rowland Hill, and not John Wesley, preached Rouquet's funeral sermons when he died the following year.

Rouquet was as busy and as outspoken as ever in the final two years of his life. In April 1775, '£507 of debts were compounded for £318, and £132 paid for 72 prisoners released'. Rouquet, Pine, Evans and Hannah More were among the subscribers. In his report Rouquet wrote, 'The discharge of such a number of useful hands must be very sensibly felt in a commercial city and the relief which their numerous families have thereby received can be no inconsiderable abatement in the poor rates of the several parishes to which they belong ... The discharge of these unfortunate persons does not amount to £1. 18. 0 per man and at this time there are not 30 prisoners in jail for debt.'[53]

In that year Rouquet's house was broken into by thieves, who stole several things of value, including a 'silver cream jug, a blue enamelled snuff box mounted in silver, three two-guinea pieces, a pair of wrought silver shoe buckles, tortoise shell ink pot mounted in silver, the silver heads of a set of casters, and a silver bougie box'. The burglars were disturbed during their raid and left a small gimlet, a borer and a broken chisel in the house. A five-guinea reward was offered, but there is no report of any of the stolen goods being recovered. This incident was reported in the press, which in itself underlines Rouquet's importance in the Bristol area.

Rouquet, always ready to struggle on behalf of liberty, was involved in the dispute surrounding the American War of Independence in 1775, which brought down on him bitter criticism. Some detested him for his 'liberal political conduct', and Tyerman claimed that he 'horrified the Bristol merchants by his ultra-radicalism and his outspoken sympathy for the revolted colonies'. In his funeral sermon, Rowland Hill defended his friend by saying he was 'the son of persecuted parents who fled from France ... for the sake of enjoying the inestimable blessings of civil and religious liberty. I mention this as an apology for his conduct in appearing so strenuous, with other great and good men, against those principles which he conceived to be in the end destructive of the liberties of mankind.'

Rouquet consistently declared himself to be loyal to the Crown and the Constitution, but that did not prevent an anonymous writer accusing him on 30 September 1775 of 'assigning the threat of unemployment for four or five hundred men in Bristol to the American war, when it was in fact caused by inability to export to Africa goods which by injudicious manufacture were unsaleable there'.[54] In his defence Rouquet wrote a long and interesting letter to *Felix Farley's Journal*, which began: 'In your journal a correspondent insinuated that Mr J[ohn] Bull had deceived me by a false account of his trade; and charges me with having asserted on his authority that in a few months the poor in this kingdom would want for bread from the American dispute.' He then quoted part of his address to the labouring and manufacturing poor:

These religious considerations I do urge upon you … to make a … lasting impression on your mind, because I have it from good authority that many … manufacturers of this city have already been, and that in all probability many will be, discharged from their employment in the course of the ensuing winter … Beware you murmur not against your superiors nor abuse your employers who may be under the painful necessity of dismissing you, from the very considerable interruption which trade has unhappily so long sustained.55

He stated that his authority for what he said was John Bull, who had repeatedly 'declared that in consequence of the suspension of trade to America he had been obliged to dismiss a great many hands and that he must dismiss many more, who were employed in the manufacture of serges for the American market'. Bull had not mentioned to Rouquet the 'ells [a measure of about 114cms] and serges made for Africa', and so had not misled him or the Bristol public.

When Rouquet had spoken of the 'deplorable situation of the poor at large almost through the kingdom', his authority had been John Wesley and not Bull. Wesley, who had travelled extensively, found the poor in most places 'to be everywhere starving for want of employment … and that whoever had given the ministry a contrary account, to make them believe that the trade and manufacture of this kingdom were generally in a flourishing state, did richly deserve to be hanged'.56

Rouquet's purpose in preaching on the subject was not to stir up 'riot, tumult and sedition', as had been reported, for his views were very different.

I fear God. I honour the king. I love my country. I revere the constitution. I mean at least to serve these several interests by considering our national distresses as a general call to repentance; and by recommending and especially to the poor every principle of piety and virtue which might promote a calm and peaceable behaviour … I did not raise the alarm. I had long ago heard much from Mr Wesley himself and from other quarters of the public distress.57

With this apology it seems that the fire of controversy was extinguished.

When only forty-six years of age Rouquet was struck down with a putrid fever, almost certainly typhus, then rife in the prisons. He suffered for about a fortnight. The evening before his speech failed he spent three or four hours in fervent prayer, when he expressed his willingness to die and was heard to pray sincerely and repeatedly for his enemies and their forgiveness before God. After a short sleep he spoke for some time from Hebrews 6:19–20, confidently expressing his hope in God and in the grace that is in Christ Jesus. A friend then asked him how it was with his soul. He placed his hand on his chest and replied, 'Peace, peace.' He told another friend that the Lord was very precious to him.

About two hours before his death Rowland Hill prayed with him, and with the weeping friends who surrounded his bed, and commended his soul into the hands of God. The last words he was heard to utter, fervently and with a view of eternity before him, were, 'I long to go home, I long to go home, I long to go home.'[58] Shortly afterwards a friend asked him to lift his hand if he felt perfectly calm and happy. He immediately lifted it. Then, silently, the cord of life was cut and he was carried home on the wings of angels. He died on Saturday 16 November 1776.

He was universally lamented. Evans in his funeral sermon, said, 'Thousands there are in this great and populous city [of Bristol] who are ready, in accents of peculiar anguish, to cry out on the sad occasion of his death. Know you not that there is a great man, an eminent, an amiable man, fallen this day in the midst of us?'[59] Even John Fletcher, not his greatest supporter, noted, 'Ro[u]quet dead and buried! The jolly man who last summer shook his head at me as at a dying man! How frail are we! God help us to live *today!* Tomorrow is the fool's day.'[60]

The funeral procession began at about eleven o'clock from his house on Kingsdown. His body was attended by a few of his select friends in five coaches and a chariot, and by thousands of mourners in the different streets through which it passed, 'whose countenances and tears expressed the feelings of their hearts'. The cortège was met in Broad Street by the charity children of St Peter's Hospital, who immediately began to sing a hymn, which they sang all the way to the church. The service was performed by Rev. Mr Barry. Six ministers supported the pall, two from the Church of

England and four from different denominations of dissenters. 'The concourse of people which attended was incredible, a very small part of whom could get into the church which was filled in a few minutes and such universal grief was scarce ever seen on the like occasion.'[61] His body was interred in the family vault in St Peter's Church.

In an appreciation of his ministry and character, Caleb Evans, in his funeral sermon for Rouquet *The Death of a Great and Good Man Lamented and Improved* on the text: 'A great man is fallen this day in Israel', called his friend, 'A man that was an example to the rich, a patron to the poor, an ornament to his profession, truly great and truly good!'[62] Rowland Hill, in his sermon *A Token of Respect to the Memory of the Late Rev. J. Rouquet*, delivered in the parish church of St Werburgh's in Bristol on Sunday 24 November 1776, the day after Rouquet's death, asked,

Where shall we discover one among the living in this city, in all respects equal to him? … Tenderness and compassion were the noble acts in which his soul delighted; I know that he preferred it to his daily food, and frequently acted as if unmerciful to himself, that he might be merciful to others. The hungry, the thirsty, the stranger, the naked, the sick and the imprisoned were sure to find a friend in him if forsaken by all besides.[63]

Both men referred to the numbers who attended the funeral. At least two elegies on his death were published, one of which was by John Clarke, who wrote:

Oh my heart bleeds. Rouquet, Rouquet is dead!
For all, who was a friend to all but kind Rouquet?

In a note he too mentioned the numbers at the funeral: 'The Muse has not exaggerated. St Peter's Bristol was so crowded … that it was with much difficulty that the corpse was got in, but as soon as it entered the church the whole congregation burst forth with such lamentation that the minister's voice could not be heard.'[64] Many others from all walks of life and from many denominations mourned his passing.

The poor and sick were always the constant object of his care and his generosity knew no bounds. Hill says he was 'generous to a fault', for he sometimes left his family short. He would borrow and even beg in order to relieve the needy. The sick often called on him, confident of his concern for them, and all who witnessed his visits 'could not but admire the faithful and affectionate way in which he dealt with them, even to a dying hour'.[65] Caleb Evans said of his dear friend that he was 'favoured with a very singular gift of visiting the sick ... Hence he became the general visitor of the sick throughout [Bristol]. The very publicans and harlots solicited his visits in their sick and dying moments,'[66] and he never neglected an opportunity of sharing Christ with them. Among his many positions of influence, he was chaplain to

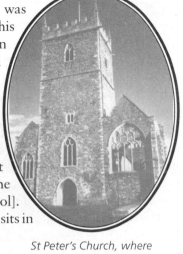

St Peter's Church, where Rouquet's body was buried in the family vault

Colston's Almshouse Chapel, where he was appointed to read prayers, and he helped to improve the unsavoury conditions in St Peter's Hospital and in the methods used to dispose of paupers' bodies.

As if to highlight his work for the sick, an advertisement appeared a month after his death for the *Bristol Dispensary*, which was originally set up for the relief of the sick and needy in their own homes, 'who might not be able to leave their families ... or for whom there was no vacancy in the public infirmary ... Now it is further proposed to extend the benefit of the institution to the delivery and relief of lying-in women and to servants and children.'[67] Rouquet's name was in the subscription list.

As a man he was warmly appreciated and loved by multitudes, who enjoyed his friendly, cheerful manner. Rowland Hill remarked that occasionally his disposition bordered too much on 'a turn of pleasantry, which might have needed a little more the spirit of solemnity'.[68] His private character testified to the genuineness of his public work. He was a devoted husband and father—'his children were not driven, but led; not alarmed, but allured into obedience'. He preferred to persuade with love than wave the rod of iron. He treated his servants with respect, as fellow-creatures who had as much right to be happy as himself. As a friend 'one more constant and sincere [Hill] never found; to have equalled him would have been difficult, to have excelled him, impossible'.[69]

In his ministry his whole desire was the salvation of souls. He therefore 'never aimed to please the ear, but to profit the heart'. He spoke to unveil the misery of fallen mankind that he might compel him to run to Christ, whom he always held up as the only remedy provided by God for salvation. 'From many hours of the most serious conversation with him,' says Hill, 'I always admired the uprightness of his heart. None could more completely detest that hateful idea, *salvation through self*; and from his inmost soul he utterly renounced every dependence, but that glorious refuge held forth for lost sinners in the gospel of Christ.'[70]

The most appropriate way to close this short biography is to quote first his friend Caleb Evans and then a more independent opinion, *Felix Farley's Bristol Journal*:

Nor will his earnestness, his zeal, his honest fervour in the discharge of the duties of his sacred function, be soon forgotten by those many precious souls that were ... convinced, converted, comforted and edified under his ministry ... The law of kindness was on his lips, fidelity, sympathy and love in his heart. In public life, it was his meat and drink to do the will of God ... How often did he appear as a *Guardian Angel* sent from heaven to bind up the broken hearted, and to comfort those that were mourning! ... From how many different quarters is this sad lamentation heard—I have lost my best friend! I have lost my patron, my benefactor, my father! ... A more truly noble catholic heart, I believe, no man ever possessed ... He lived not for himself but others, he spent and was spent in labours of piety and love ... His native genius, his peculiar gifts, and above all his piety and warm benevolence of heart, conspired to render him a great man.[71]

[Rouquet's] character as a man, a Christian and a clergyman has seldom been excelled. Humane, generous, disinterested, compassionate—almost to excess. He was eyes to the blind, feet to the lame; and caused thousands of drooping hearts to sing for joy. As a husband, a parent, a friend, malice itself cannot withhold her praise. His assiduity, his zeal, his fervour in the discharge of his various clerical duties, his parishioners, the numerous attendants on his weekly lectures, the old and the orphan young of the hospital to which he was chaplain, the prisoners (to whom he was ever a faithful preacher … and … comforter), the poor, the distressed of every class (who in the most abject circumstances looked to him as their common patron and father), his friends, his foes and the city in general can amply testify 'Blessed is that servant whom his Lord when he comes shall find so doing.'[72]

Endnotes

1 **Caleb Evans,** *The Death of a Great and Good Man Lamented and Improved* (Bristol, 1776), p. 16n.
2 *Ibid.,* pp. 16–17.
3 *Ibid.,* p. 17.
4 *Ibid.,* pp. 17–18.
5 **Charles Wesley,** *The Journal of Charles Wesley* (Grand Rapids, Baker Book House, 1908 reprint), vol. 2, p. 15.
6 **Evans,** *The Death of a Great and Good Man,* p.18.
7 **A. Barrett Sackett,** *James Rouquet and his Part in Early Methodism* (The Wesley Historical Society, 1972), p. 2.
8 *Arminian Magazine,* 1779, vol.2.
9 **John Wesley,** *The Works of John Wesley* (Grand Rapids, Baker Book House, 1998 reprint), vol. 2, p. 151.
10 **Arthur Glendinning Ives,** *Kingswood School in Wesley's Day and Since* (London, Epworth Press, 1970), p. 46.
11 **Wesley,** *Works,* vol. 2, p. 301.
12 **Evans,** *The Death of a Great and Good Man,* p. 18.
13 **A.C.H. Seymour,** *The Life and Times of Selina Countess of Huntingdon* (Stoke-on-Trent, Tentmaker, 2000 reprint), vol. 2, p. 36.
14 **Sackett,** *James Rouquet,* p. 5.
15 **Evans,** *The Death of a Great and Good Man,* p. 20n.
16 *Ibid.,* p. 18.
17 **Rowland Hill,** *A Token of Respect to the Memory of the Late Rev. J. Rouquet* (Bristol, 1776), pp. 15–16.
18 *Proceedings of the Wesley Historical Society,* vol. 27, p. 61.
19 **John Wesley,** *The Letters of John Wesley* (London, Epworth Press, 1931), vol. 4, pp. 10–11.
20 **Sackett,** *James Rouquet,* pp. 8–9.
21 **Wesley,** *Works,* vol. 3, pp. 33–34.

22 Seymour, *Countess of Huntingdon,* vol. 1, p. 596n.

23 *Ibid.*

24 Sackett, *James Rouquet,* p. 16.

25 Wesley, *Letters,* vol. 4, p. 142.

26 *Ibid.,* pp. 142–143.

27 Sackett, *James Rouquet,* p. 10.

28 *Arminian Magazine,* vol. 5, p. 105.

29 Evans, *The Death of a Great and Good Man,* p. 19.

30 Sackett, *James Rouquet,* p. 6.

31 Evans, *The Death of a Great and Good Man,* p. 19n.

32 *Ibid.,* p. 19.

33 Hill, *J. Rouquet,* p. 21n.

34 Sackett, *James Rouquet,* p. 11.

35 *Ibid.,* p. 19.

36 Wesley, *Works,* vol. 12, p. 410.

37 Evans, *The Death of a Great and Good Man,* pp. 19–20.

38 Sackett, *James Rouquet,* p. 15.

39 Seymour, *Countess of Huntingdon,* vol. 2, p. 37n.

40 Sackett, *James Rouquet,* p. 12.

41 By a Gentleman, *Some Particulars of the Life and Death of Jonathan Britain* (Bristol, 1772), pp. iii–iv.

42 William Talbot, *The Rev. Mr Talbot's Narrative of the Whole of his Proceedings Relative to Jonathan Britain* (Bristol, 1772), pp. 15–16.

43 Sackett, *James Rouquet,* p. 12.

44 Luke Tyerman, *Wesley's Designated Successor* (London, Hodder & Stoughton, 1882), p. 243.

45 Wesley, *Works,* vol. 12, p. 140.

46 Sackett, *James Rouquet,* p. 12.

47 *Ibid.,* p. 13.

48 Wesley, *Works,* vol. 12, p. 143.

49 Wesley, *Letters,* vol. 6, p. 189.

50 Luke Tyerman, *The Life and Times of John Wesley* (London, Hodder & Stoughton, 1890), vol. 3, p. 189.

51 Sackett, *James Rouquet,* p. 27.

52 Tyerman, *Wesley's Designated Successor,* p. 355.

53 Sackett, *James Rouquet,* p. 14.

54 *Ibid.*, pp. 24–25.

55 *Ibid.*, p. 25.

56 *Ibid.*, pp. 25–26.

57 *Ibid.*, p. 26.

58 Hill, *J. Rouquet,* p. 25.

59 Evans, *The Death of a Great and Good Man,* p. 16.

60 Tyerman, *Wesley's Designated Successor,* p. 366.

61 Sackett, *James Rouquet,* p. 28.

62 Evans, *The Death of a Great and Good Man,* p. 27.

63 Hill, *J. Rouquet,* p. 15.

64 *Ibid.*, p. 29.

65 Hill, *J. Rouquet,* p. 17.

66 Evans, *The Death of a Great and Good Man,* p. 21n.

67 Sackett, *James Rouquet,* p. 14.

68 Hill, *J. Rouquet,* pp. 20–21.

69 *Ibid.*, pp. 19–20.

70 *Ibid.*, p. 23.

71 Evans, *The Death of a Great and Good Man,* pp. 20–23.

72 Sackett, *James Rouquet,* p. 28.

Captain Jonathan Scott

In the Lord's army

Jonathan Scott was born at Betton Strange, Shrewsbury, on 15 November 1735. He was the second son of Richard and Elizabeth Scott. Richard was a younger son of Scott of Scott's Hall, Kent, while Elizabeth was the eldest daughter and sole heiress of Jonathan Scott of Betton. Both on his father's and his mother's side he could trace 'his ancestry to the brother of John Baliol, king of the Scots,[1] some four centuries earlier, and through him to the Norman family which came over at the Conquest'.[2] The family was known as Baliol le Scott until for brevity and convenience they dropped the Baliol and became simply Scott.

Richard Scott was a military officer, who rose to the rank of captain in the Buffs in the British Army. After an ordinary education Jonathan followed in his father's footsteps and joined the army at 16 as a cornet, and in time was promoted to captain-lieutenant in the Seventh Queen's Own Dragoons. He remained in the army for seventeen years and saw three campaigns in Europe, probably fought at Warburg in Germany when only twenty-four, and was present at the Battle of Minden in 1759, when English forces routed the French—a turning point in the Seven Years' War. However, as he was a cavalryman of the right wing of the allied army commanded by Lord George Sackville, he took no part in the fighting.

John de Baliol, king of Scotland from 1292 to 1296, from whose brother Captain Scott could trace his ancestry

His early army career was a life of dissipation and he enjoyed the vices common among his fellow soldiers. Yet, at the same time, the danger to which he was constantly exposed was seriously impressed on his mind.

Captain Jonathan Scott

This in turn led him to experience 'religious fits', as he termed them. At the beginning of these 'fits' he made a resolution to live a strict and pious life for about a month, reasoning that if he could keep his resolution for that length of time, he should be able to persevere for longer. However, as with all acts of self-righteousness, he failed, and before the end of the month he gave in to temptation and all his hard work came to nothing. His hopes vanished and he was left in great distress.

Throughout this time it was his daily practice to read the Psalms and lessons of the day, a toilsome duty in his own mind, and one which his fellow officers suffered without malice, mainly because in all other respects his behaviour was just like theirs. 'Well, Scott,' they used to ask, 'have you read your Psalms and lessons today?' During one of these readings he came across the words of David, 'Seven times a day will I praise thee.' Immediately he thought he had discovered the reason for his failed resolutions, and set about praying to God seven times a day, fully believing that now he would be able to persevere. Once again he was disappointed.

He knew something was wrong with his life and his self-imposed religion, but did not know what it was, or how to rectify it. He felt his spiritual poverty deeply. Occasionally, he omitted his religious duties altogether, for he recognised the uselessness of them and their hypocrisy, as he desired to follow the very lusts of his heart against which he prayed. On the one hand he wanted to be religious, on the other he knew he had no power to resist the sinful propensities that frequently overpowered him.

While serving with his regiment, he was stationed in a town where there had been a bequest of religious books, to be distributed without charge to every soldier who should pass through that place. Scott, having heard of the bequest, begged the commander of the regiment to acquire these books for his officers and men, arguing that they might do them a great deal of good, or at least could do them no harm. The commander agreed. Upon receiving his own copy he quickly retired to his room to read it. While alone, he used a form of prayer that he found in the book, and which concluded with the words, 'for Jesus' sake'. On repeating the name of Jesus, he was seized with the most extraordinary feelings—feelings he could not describe and which were so sweet to his soul he could never forget. In a state of ecstasy he was compelled to say over and over again, 'for Jesus' sake, for Jesus' sake, for Jesus' sake'.

Sometime before his conversion he was riding near Shrewsbury, when his horse fell, throwing him from the saddle in such a manner that he partially dislocated his neck. Providentially a stranger with medical skills happened to be passing by and seeing the situation immediately went to Scott's aid. He managed to reset the neck and so saved Scott from serious injury and possibly death. Looking back to this accident the captain always gave thanks to God for preserving his life.

When quartered in or near Brighton, he went out shooting and a furious storm arose. Remembering that in the vicinity lived a farmer, with whom some of his regiment's horses had been left to graze, he hurried to his house for shelter. He was welcomed by the farmer, a godly man, who soon invited him to accompany him to Ote Hall, one of Lady Huntingdon's chapels, to hear William Romaine, whom he represented as an extraordinary minister. Scott, at the time in one of his 'religious fits', agreed. At the church he was immediately struck by the neatness and solemnity of the congregation, as well as the impressive manner in which the prayers were read. Romaine preached from John 14:6, 'I am the way ...', and the word flew like an arrow into his heart. 'This,' he said to himself, 'this is the thing, the very thing I want, and have wanted so long, and knew not what it was, or how to obtain it.'[3] In relating his conversion to two friends many years later, he said his mind had been fully prepared to receive the gospel, so that the instant he heard it, he embraced it wholeheartedly.

After hearing the sermon and reaping so much benefit from it, he was naturally eager to talk with the preacher. He rode with him from Ote Hall, joined him for some refreshment at a nearby house, and tried every way to converse with him, but to no avail. Romaine remained shy and distant. Some time after this, Scott had to travel to Shrewsbury, and passing through London, the thought came to him to call on Romaine, to see whether there was any difference

William Romaine, under whose preaching Scott was converted

between the air of London and that of Brighton, to use his own expression. To his great surprise, he was received in a most friendly manner by the great preacher, who talked with him in a warm and profitable way, before praying affectionately with and for him.

As they parted Romaine asked Scott if he would pass on a letter to Thomas Powys of Berwick in Shropshire, who at the time was entertaining Henry Venn. Leaving London in the Shrewsbury mail-coach, he found himself sitting next to a major bound for Shrewsbury. In the course of their conversation Scott asked if the major knew any families in that town. The major answered that he knew the Scotts fairly well. The captain, whose interest was heightened by the reply, begged to know more, hoping his own name would be mentioned. Various particulars were recounted by the major, but with no reference to the captain himself. On further questioning, the major said, 'Yes—there was one mad fellow, who many years ago went into the army; and, when he was there, turned Methodist, and went about preaching with the regiment.' Soon they arrived at Oxford and were ushered into a room lighted by two large candles. The captain immediately took hold of both candles, one in each hand, and walked up to the major. He bowed and said, 'Give me leave, sir, to introduce to you the mad Captain Scott!' The major was rightly embarrassed. Scott assured him he had not taken offence, and asked him, when in Shropshire, to correct the rumour that he was deranged. He then had the opportunity of sharing the gospel with the major, who agreed with everything that was said. This was the first and only time Scott spoke to the major and he never found out if their conversation had produced any lasting good in him.[4]

After a few days with his family and friends, Scott rode early in the morning to Berwick to deliver Romaine's letter. On that same morning, soon after breakfast and family prayer, Thomas Powys, his wife and Henry Venn were in the kitchen looking out over the front lawn, when they saw the captain, dressed in his uniform and riding towards the house. As soon as Powys recognised him, and unaware of Scott's conversion, he said, 'There is Captain Scott. What can he want here? I am determined not to see him if I can avoid it.' He then quickly withdrew.

Scott rode up to the house and asked the servant, 'Is Mr Powys at home?' The servant, not realising his master's reluctance to see his uninvited guest,

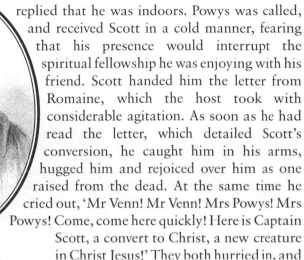
Henry Venn, one of Scott's good friends

replied that he was indoors. Powys was called, and received Scott in a cold manner, fearing that his presence would interrupt the spiritual fellowship he was enjoying with his friend. Scott handed him the letter from Romaine, which the host took with considerable agitation. As soon as he had read the letter, which detailed Scott's conversion, he caught him in his arms, hugged him and rejoiced over him as one raised from the dead. At the same time he cried out, 'Mr Venn! Mr Venn! Mrs Powys! Mrs Powys! Come, come here quickly! Here is Captain Scott, a convert to Christ, a new creature in Christ Jesus!' They both hurried in, and being informed of the contents of Romaine's letter, all three embraced the penitent with heavenly joy.

The change in Scott was apparent immediately. He made new friends and engaged in new pursuits. One of his new friends, Henry Venn, soon wrote to him a long letter of encouragement, with directions for leading a Christian life. His letter is dated 6 November 1765 and opens, 'I cannot leave Shropshire without giving you joy on your knowledge of Christ, and determination to live in his service.' He then sets out a 'few hints, furnished from long service in the Church of Christ':

Your Christian calling is a warfare, where no quarter can be given on either side. If you prove faithful unto death … the Redeemer's presence will be your heaven for evermore. Should you forsake his service, or hold secret correspondence with his foes, you must be punished, like them, with eternal infamy in hell.

The enemies you have to oppose, and conquer, will probably be, first, your former intimates, friends and nearest relations, whose polite conversation and affection for you have been so pleasing: for till their judgment of sin, true religion, and man's chief good, are formed from Scripture, as your own now is, they must both despise and hate the way of life in which you must persist. With these opposers your corrupt nature will take part, and a subtle destroyer, long practised in arts and wiles, to compass the ruin of immortal souls. In this perilous condition you have joined yourself (effectually influenced by his grace) to Christ, as your Leader and Commander. Under his banner, diligently using the MEANS he, in tenderest love, enjoins, you are confidently to expect both protection and victory.

The 'means' Venn highlights are: secret prayer, devout study of the Bible, public worship, hearing faithful preachers, fellowshipping with other Christians, and much retirement for spiritual meditation and reflection. He concludes by saying,

With respect to the multitude of ignorant and licentious men, you must expect their ridicule and censure; which by no means should gall or irritate your mind. You could not be a servant of Christ, were you approved by them … Love will enable you meekly to receive contemptuous treatment, and hard speeches against your faith, your conduct, and your friends. Be not eager to justify yourself, nor over-forward to make converts by much speaking: an irksome truth becomes more so by being unseasonably urged … But in victory over pride, anger, and all wickedness—in steadfastly observing every rule of holy living laid down by our Saviour—in courteous behaviour to all men—in calmly urging the Word of God, when some favourable opportunity occurs bearing testimony to the truth—in these things you cannot exceed. Wait patiently; and you will, by such irreproachable and wise conduct, stop the mouth of prejudice, and win over some to come forth and live a Christian life, as you do.

I wish you much of the presence and peace of God in your soul; in your practice and tempers, much steadiness and love; and a gracious answer to your prayers for your friends, relations, and fellow-sinners. May we remember each other before God; beseeching him, that we may strongly recommend his truth and service, by great usefulness, till we are for ever with him![5]

Following such wise counsel, his language, desires and hopes all focused on his Saviour. In a letter to a friend, dated 20 March 1766, he writes, 'God is ever watchful over me, and keeps my soul alive and vigilant amidst the dangers that surround me. This peculiar goodness to me raises in me the comfortable belief that the Lord is with me, and will, in good time, teach me more of his will, and enable me, from time to time, to do it.'[6]

Initially it seems that his fellow soldiers put up with his 'religious mania', much to his disappointment, for he writes in a careful hand,

I have not yet been attacked by any of the officers in the regiment, nor had one single word said to me, but have been suffered to do what I please; but I do not expect that Satan will let them be long silent, but will stir his people up against me; indeed, if he does not I shall begin to be alarmed and suspect that he does not hate me so much as I hope he ever will have cause to do, and undoubtedly will if I hate myself and love my adorable Jesus as much as I ought to do. God grant therefore that soon open hostilities may commence betwixt us and last as long as I remain on earth. And here let me entreat, my dear friend, pray to God for me that I may be enabled to go forth in the strength of the Lord and to fight the good fight of faith manfully under Christ's banner, who is the glorious Captain of my Salvation, my Almighty Chief and Leader, that I may be his faithful soldier and follower, then I am sure to come off more than conqueror.[7]

Scott did not have long to wait for opposition to arise. Before he had left his regiment to travel to Shrewsbury, he had been suspected of religious enthusiasm, especially as he attended the ministry of such a notorious preacher as Romaine and associated with other Christians. When he rejoined his regiment, his former companions were convinced that he had become an 'arrant Methodist', and shunned his company, much to his relief. He could no longer stand their idle conversation and obscenities, and was shocked to hear the blasphemous oaths they uttered. But as his old associates turned their backs on him, God gave him a dear Christian friend, with whom he lodged. Scott calls him 'a faithful brother in Christ: the adjutant of the regiment, Mr Barrett; he is a most gracious child of God indeed'.[8] 'We strive to assist, comfort, and help each other on our way towards the promised heavenly Canaan, all in our power; and the Lord is very gracious to us, and blesses us greatly to each other. How ought I to praise the Lord for this great blessing—this dear friend! with whom I talk and sing of our dear Jesus' redeeming love!'[9]

In August 1766 he travelled to Olney and heard 'two excellent discourses from Mr Newton. What a monument of the mercy and free grace of God is he, and still, my dear friend [Richard Hill], I think there is not so great a one on earth as myself.' He was obviously delighted with what he found at

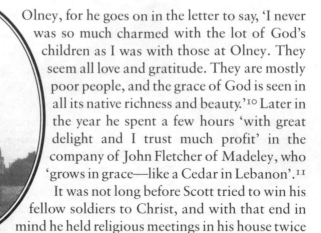

Olney parish church, where
Scott visited in 1766

Olney, for he goes on in the letter to say, 'I never was so much charmed with the lot of God's children as I was with those at Olney. They seem all love and gratitude. They are mostly poor people, and the grace of God is seen in all its native richness and beauty.'[10] Later in the year he spent a few hours 'with great delight and I trust much profit' in the company of John Fletcher of Madeley, who 'grows in grace—like a Cedar in Lebanon'.[11]

It was not long before Scott tried to win his fellow soldiers to Christ, and with that end in mind he held religious meetings in his house twice a day in 1766 for any soldier who cared to attend. He replied enthusiastically to Richard Hill, who had invited him to visit Henry Venn, 'I hope and trust the Lord is extending his mercy and grace still further in our regiment, as there seems to be a desire amongst some of our men to wait upon the Lord, and to seek after him ... To attend to this as long as such a poor creature as I am is in the least made serviceable, is undoubtedly my first duty.'[12] He loved to tell others what wonderful things God had done for him, and on 17 December 1766, he wrote,

To the praise of his free grace, I must invite all that fear the Lord, to come and hear what great things he has done for my soul. He has plucked my feet out of the net, he has broken my bonds, and set my happy soul at liberty. O how good and gracious is the Lord to such an unworthy wretch! But worthy is the Lamb that was slain; in him is my merit; in him is my worthiness. This, and this only, will I mention and make my boast.[13]

It was in Leicester, probably late in 1766, that Scott first began to preach. A godly person, to whom he was introduced and who had heard about the meetings he held, led him into a kitchen and left him with only a Bible, a hymn book and his God, informing him that he must preach there that evening. He consented and many years later was told by a respectable friend that on coming to Leicester, he found several godly Christians, who were the fruits of his ministry. Scott himself said on 3 January 1767, 'I hope the Lord is at work here [in Leicester], though by the meanest, weakest, and unworthiest of all instruments. But it is all his own work, therefore he can work by the weakest means, or without any. Be all praise and glory given to his great name!'[14] Fletcher, writing to Lady Huntingdon, said, 'For some months he has exhorted his dragoons daily; for some weeks he has preached publicly at Leicester in the Methodist meet-house, in his regimentals, to numerous congregations, with good success. The stiff regular ones pursue him with hue and cry, but I believe he is quite beyond their reach.'[15]

In February 1767 George Whitefield wrote to him,

I must again welcome him [Captain Scott] into the field of battle. I must entreat him to keep his rank as a captain, and not suffer any persuasions to influence him to descend to the lower degree of a common soldier. If God shall choose a red coat preacher, who shall say unto him, 'What doest thou?' ... Blessed be the Captain of our salvation for drafting out young champions to reconnoitre and attack the enemy. You will beat the march in every letter and bid the common soldiers not halt, but go forward.[16]

Three months later he was preaching for Fletcher, who wrote to Whitefield with an enthusiastic report. 'Last Sunday seven-night, Captain Scott preached to my congregation a sermon, which was more blessed, though preached only upon my horse-block, than a hundred of those I preach in the pulpit.'[17] On the Monday he preached in Madeley wood to a huge crowd, many of whom were curious to see the preaching captain. In September of the same year he joined Whitefield and Lady Huntingdon at Leeds, where he preached to 'amazing crowds'. Seymour comments that his 'popularity was very great at this period. Many of the rich, worldly wise

John Fletcher of Madeley, an enthusiastic supporter of Captain Scott and honourable could not endure such preaching; but the common people heard him gladly, and blessed God for the preaching, which they could fully understand.'[18]

While in the army he made the most of every opportunity, preaching in York, Manchester and other places to which his military duty called. At Berwick, he was invited to preach by the mayor of the town, who obtained a place of worship for him. On approaching the chapel he saw that the mayor's servants were stationed at the door to keep out the mob, but to this he strongly objected. He was commissioned to preach the gospel to 'every creature' and insisted that everyone should be allowed to hear him proclaim the good news. At Manchester his preaching resulted in the conversion of two people: one a lady, who went to hear him because she had seen the service advertised in a newspaper; and the other a gentleman, who heard him in a timber yard. The latter soon afterwards settled at Stone in Staffordshire, where he encouraged a gospel interest.

It is apparent that during 1767 he was under pressure to leave the army. His 'religious doings' had angered his commanding officer, who was determined to deprive him of his commission. In August of that year he wrote to John Newton, and gave him an interesting account of an interview he had had with General Howard, the colonel of the regiment. After a dinner given by the colonel, Scott was summoned to talk about his preaching. The colonel had been told that Scott had perverted some of the soldiers into adopting his way of thinking. He said it was not right to influence the weak and ignorant in such ways, and that everyone's religion should be kept to themselves.

Scott admitted he had preached. He also asked the colonel if he had in any way neglected his duty as an officer, or if the men he had 'perverted' had neglected theirs. General Howard confessed that he was more diligent than before his religious turn and that the men were good soldiers, but in his view 'stupid'. Scott said that the soldiers he had talked to were changed for the better. He then appealed that he should have the same right to serve God 'without molestation', as others had 'to run into every excess, provided they did not break the laws of their country, or the rules of the service'. He concluded by saying that in religious matters he would only be guided by the authority of the Bible.

In the course of their conversation, and with the intrepidity of spirit that marked his ministry, he observed to Newton that

… it came into my way to take notice of some oaths that were sworn during our being together after dinner, and some obscene talk, upon which I left the company. The general was one of the transgressors. I reminded him of it, and told him why I left. He confessed it was wrong; and so, after having on both sides hoped that there had been nothing said that had given offence, we parted very good friends, or seemingly so, he confessing he had nothing else to lay to my charge.[19]

John Newton, one of Scott's correspondents

On 1 June 1768 Scott married Elizabeth Clay of Wollerton, near Market Drayton in Shropshire. Elizabeth was a godly woman, and much of her time was spent in prayer. According to Dugald Macfadyen she possessed 'all the virtues and other assets with which eminent ladies in the eighteenth century were so singularly endowed— eminent piety, remarkable prudence, a handsome estate, economical habits and an affectionate disposition'.[20] She proved to be a most suitable wife, who supported wholeheartedly the ministry of her husband.

Scott was happy to remain in the army as long as he could use the opportunities that arose to preach the gospel. However, some of his superiors were uncomfortable with his religion, perhaps suspecting divided allegiance, and one of them advised him to leave. After carefully considering the best course of action, he sold his commission on 16 March 1769, and from that time dedicated himself to the ministry of the word among the dissenters. 'My heart is as much with you, I trust,' wrote Newton in 1769, after hearing about his decision, 'as it would be had you the most canonical appointment and the most regular sphere of service. And I would as willingly hear you in your usual places as if you preached in St Paul's.'[21]

Leaving the army was not an easy decision, for he was well qualified for a military command, and might have enjoyed all the trappings of high rank. Before his conversion his highest ambition had been to become one of the illustrious heroes of his country, but the great Sovereign of the world had destined him, not for worldly honour, but for the highest honour and service of all—preaching Christ. From this point he turned his back on the applause of men to seek the glory of God.

After getting married he lived in his wife's home at Wollerton, where he gathered a congregation. (Much later, about 1800, soon after his wife's death, the first chapel and manse were built from a gift of £300 from Mrs Scott's will.) From his Wollerton base he embarked on evangelistic tours, which contributed to the founding of twenty-two Congregational churches in Shropshire, Staffordshire, Cheshire and Lancashire. On occasions he rode into a town in the full uniform of a captain-lieutenant of his majesty's dragoons, gathered a crowd, and without compromise preached the gospel to them. If a riot threatened, as sometimes happened, he threw back his cloak to reveal the splendour of his 'regimentals' and commanded all and sundry to listen to his message in the name of King George III.

Soon after his settlement at Wollerton, he preached at Market Drayton, where the open air services had been repeatedly interrupted by hooligans. The small company of believers had been sheltered by a brave Welsh woman, Elizabeth Vernon, whose windows were broken by the mob when they met on her premises. Scott travelled to Drayton to help them and conducted the meetings in person for some time. He secured a site, erected a building and organized them into a strong church, made up chiefly of men and women converted through his ministry. The chapel was formally constituted in 1776 and described as a 'meeting house of Protestant Christians of the Independent persuasion'. It had twenty-eight members, and Scott drew up its covenant and articles of belief. He regarded this congregation as his own particular people.

He introduced the gospel to Newport, Shropshire, where he built a chapel on land that had been given to him in 1765 by Thomas Jones, one of six students sent down from St Edmund Hall, Oxford, because they had 'offered free prayer, had connected themselves with "Methodists", had attended unlawful religious meetings and had expounded the Scriptures not being in Holy Orders'. A chapel was built, but the work failed to flourish and the meeting place was soon closed. In 1792 Moses Silvester, 'an earnest and resolute' Christian, settled in business at Newport. He revived the work, and on his promise to keep the pulpit well supplied with suitable preachers, Scott transferred the chapel to him. Two other churches in the county, at Wistanswick and Ollerton, owed their existence to Scott. He preached for them in the early years, and his wife left them an endowment of £300, which was later lost by the negligence of her trustees.

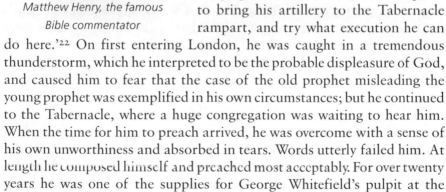

Matthew Henry, the famous Bible commentator

In 1770 he began to visit Chester and the Queen Street congregation that had seceded from the church where the famous Matthew Henry had once been minister, because two successive ministers had fallen into Socinianism. Scott often supplied for two or three Sundays at a time. His ministry was very popular and several were converted under his preaching. In 1772 a church was formed and William Armitage became the minister, and he and Scott became lifelong friends.

He also travelled to places further afield. Both Romaine and Whitefield invited him to London, the latter saying to the Tabernacle congregation, 'I have invited the captain to bring his artillery to the Tabernacle rampart, and try what execution he can do here.'[22] On first entering London, he was caught in a tremendous thunderstorm, which he interpreted to be the probable displeasure of God, and caused him to fear that the case of the old prophet misleading the young prophet was exemplified in his own circumstances; but he continued to the Tabernacle, where a huge congregation was waiting to hear him. When the time for him to preach arrived, he was overcome with a sense of his own unworthiness and absorbed in tears. Words utterly failed him. At length he composed himself and preached most acceptably. For over twenty years he was one of the supplies for George Whitefield's pulpit at the Tabernacle. Arnold Dallimore states that along with Torial Joss, another

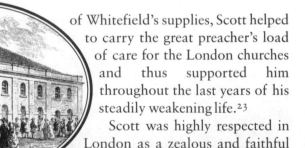

George Whitefield's Tabernacle, Moorfields, where Captain Scott occasionally preached

of Whitefield's supplies, Scott helped to carry the great preacher's load of care for the London churches and thus supported him throughout the last years of his steadily weakening life.[23]

Scott was highly respected in London as a zealous and faithful preacher, who was devoted to the cause of Christ. In a letter he wrote on 9 November 1773, a few days after one of his visits to London, he describes his congregations and the encouraging progress of the gospel.

I hope the Lord is doing great things in and for poor lost sinners, by the means of his glorious gospel. At least, if we may judge from appearances, such as most crowded, serious, attentive, and affected audiences; and these not only upon particular occasions, but for a constancy; and likewise from the many notes put up by persons under distress of soul to the minister, to pray for them; and from the many fresh applications there are from divers places to come over and help them. All these things look as if the harvest was great.[24]

In June 1773 he first preached to a thousand hearers in Stoke-on-Trent, and in December he began a series of visits to Lancaster, which lasted for three years. He loved the people there and considered them a sincere and godly folk, with 'good large hearts'. He usually stayed with them for two or three months at a time. From Lancaster he visited Ulverston, Garstang, and other places in the vicinity. He introduced the gospel into some of these places and on many occasions his preaching was eminently blessed by God. On 11 February 1774, he wrote to a friend with encouraging news of what the Lord was doing in and around Lancaster. 'I hope, I may in truth tell you the good news, that the Lord is abundantly blessing his word in and about this place. I have had several doors opened to preach; some in the country west of Preston … where, at present, there is the most pleasing and promising prospect of much good, through the divine blessing, being done.'[25] Quite a number in those parts were converted through his ministry.

In 1774 he was offered the pastorate of High Street at Lancaster, but after seeking God and listening to the counsel of a few Christian friends, he declined. With the view of being able to administer the Lord's Supper, he was ordained on 18 September 1776 in the church at Lancaster, not as pastor, but as a presbyter or teacher.

When he visited Elswick in 1774 the Independent minister, who had no sympathy with the views or methods of the evangelical revival, refused to unlock the chapel doors. Eventually the trustees forced open the doors and Scott preached to a large congregation. Scott's work there soon led to the departure of the unhappy pastor, who was replaced by an evangelist of Scott's choice, who in turn became the minister of the church.

Two years later Scott began to preach in the open air at Newcastle-under-Lyme, Staffordshire, and the following year, after gathering converts, a church was formed. Seven years later he bought a piece of derelict ground and built a chapel on it. He also travelled to Leek, where he initiated a lawsuit to regain a meeting house that had fallen into the hands of Unitarians; to Stone, where a gospel work had been started by the gentleman who had heard him preach in a Manchester timber yard; and to Uttoxeter, where he was present at the opening of a new chapel.

On 18 June 1777, Henry Venn wrote to his son from Bath and told him of Captain Scott's progress in the gospel. Referring to Scott and his wife, he remarks on how they 'set out in the way to glory long, long after me' and 'how they have got beyond me!' In the letter he mentions that Scott had said to him recently, 'It was worth while for us to come to Bristol, if it had been only to suffer as we have done under the kind hand of our Lord; for now we can tell of his faithfulness and consolations, which we related before upon hearsay.' Venn also says that Scott's wife 'was two months at the point of death' and how Scott himself 'has been cut for a cancer, the disease which killed his father'.[26]

Scott opened a meeting house at Nantwich, a work that Whitefield had begun twenty-seven years before. In 1780 a handful of people, 'led by a joiner and a shoemaker, hired a painter's shop from a sympathetic Quaker, fitted it with two pews, some forms and a pulpit, and invited Jonathan

Scott to open their humble meeting place'.[27] It was some time before the church could support a minister, so, with the help of Armitage and other neighbouring ministers, Scott often conducted the Sunday services. He kept in close contact with the people right up to his death and his visits greatly encouraged them.

While he was preaching in Hanley, Staffordshire, two or three people from Congleton travelled the twelve miles across the Cheshire border to hear him and invited him to preach in their town. He accepted the invitation and, as there was no building in which to minister, preached either in the street or in the yard of the inn where he was staying. Rowland Hill, who happened to be in the neighbourhood, preached there the following Sunday also in the open air. Scott was so encouraged by the effects of the gospel that at his own expense he fitted out a room for worship, where he or the supplies he organized could preach. The work of God prospered so much that ten years later, in 1790, again mainly at his own expense, he built a chapel in Mill Street.

In 1789 William Maurice, minister at Stockport, registered a house for preaching at Middlewich and three years later a chapel was built. Scott was one of the preachers on the opening day, which was marred by riots and many of the worshippers were attacked—all at the instigation of 'Parson Adams', the notorious incumbent of the parish church. Scott always maintained his interest in the work at Middlewich and visited the town on many occasions. He was also interested in Northwich, where the dissenting cause was very weak. He persuaded Job Wilson, 'a man of primitive simplicity and apostolic zeal', to leave Northowram Academy, where he had been training for the ministry for only six weeks, and to take charge of the work at Northwich. The move was a complete success. Wilson built up a strong church and remained there for the forty-one years of his ministerial life. One historian, who refers to Scott as 'the Whitefield of Cheshire', remarks that one of his best blessings to Cheshire was the gift, under God, of Job Wilson.

A small group of Christians in Macclesfield were forced to move their meeting place on several occasions. Once they rented and furnished a barn for worship, but after three weeks were turned out into the street by the clergyman owner. When they started to build their own meeting place the minister departed suddenly, leaving them with a half-completed chapel and no funds to finish it. They appealed to Congregationalists in Manchester and Cheshire for help and, as the minute books for the church record, were greatly assisted by Scott.

We were afterwards supplied with ministers from different places till the Lord sent, to our great assistance, the Rev Mr Scott of Drayton in Shropshire (better known as Captain Scott) ... Mr Scott ordered, at his own expense, the communion pew to be made, and twelve pews next to the same; the chapel being finished with forms or benches by the Manchester friends. The Lord's kindness in raising this congregation such a kind friend in the Rev Mr Scott, we hope will be gratefully remembered by us and by our posterity.[28]

After the chapel was completed, Scott travelled from Wollerton to preside at the first Lord's Supper, and thereafter gave his new-found friends every assistance. Apparently, when Scott rode into town in his full regimentals to preach, half the population turned out to hear him. When the first settled minister died in 1789, he preached his funeral sermon, and recommended to them as a replacement a Mr Wildbore, who became their second minister. In December 1796, he passed on cautious but wise counsel to them concerning the settlement of another minister, Daniel Dunkerley, who had been preaching for them.

I am glad Mr Dunkerley is so well liked. I have not the pleasure of knowing him; having never, that I recollect, seen him. I hear nothing but good of him; therefore 'twill be well to engage him to supply you for some time. Perhaps it may be better for him to go and return as he does at present, than to quite leave his business. I think preachers should take such an important step deliberately; and a people not be hasty in persuading to such a measure; for if we draw anyone out of certain bread, we are bound to maintain those who leave it for our sakes—that is, if they behave well.[29]

Dunkerley was ordained in August 1798.

It was about 1779 that Scott became friendly with Lady Glenorchy, a godly woman of considerable property. Thanks to the influence of Rowland Hill, she was a keen supporter of the evangelical party. At the time she was looking for a man of God who would help distribute her many charitable gifts and Scott was recommended to her. He advised her to make provision for a theological education so that the many vacancies that were arising could be filled by trained men, and for evangelistic tours. Several young men were prepared for the ministry at Edward Williams's Academy, Oswestry, at her ladyship's expense, and then at its successor, Newcastle-under-Lyme under John Whitridge. While at Oswestry the students occasionally assisted Scott, and some of them worked in the same capacity after they had finished their studies.

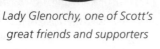

Lady Glenorchy liberally contributed to the support of her ministers who did not receive adequate salaries from their congregations, and also helped to finance various chapels that Scott erected. On a journey to Buxton she reached Matlock and could not find a suitable place to worship. So she purchased a small house, with a small but derelict chapel nearby that could seat three hundred people, and immediately gave them to Scott.

The congregation at Hanley, built up from the converts of Scott, who had first preached from a horse block at the lower end of High Street, was regularly supplied by one of Lady Glenorchy's students as well as by Scott. In 1783 they formed a church and in the following year a chapel was built with galleries on three sides. The building was registered as a 'place of public worship for Protestant dissenters of the Independent persuasion' on 15 January 1784. Two years later Scott settled James Boden as their pastor and he exercised a useful ministry there for twelve years, admitting 135 persons into fellowship during that time. Scott also supported Boden in extension work at Stafford and at his own expense provided a minister when a new chapel was opened. In the same county a chapel was opened at Cheadle in 1800 with Scott's encouragement and support.

Lady Glenorchy, one of Scott's great friends and supporters

In the year that Boden became the pastor of Hanley, Scott was deeply saddened by the death of Lady Glenorchy. Writing to a friend on 2 October 1786, he mourned, 'The death of my invaluable friend, the truly excellent Lady Glenorchy, greatly affected me. I know not her fellow left behind, dear Lady Huntingdon excepted. I cannot but be affected with and mourn for my own and Zion's great loss; but her work was done ... May we, as she was, be full of the fruits of righteousness; and soon we shall be with her before the throne above!'[30] Lady Glenorchy, who had said of Scott that his conversation and preaching had 'ever been a reviving cordial to my soul', bequeathed to her trusted friend £5000 'for the education of young men for the ministry and other religious purposes', and among other bequests left him the chapel and house she had purchased at Matlock. Scott moved to Matlock in 1794, where the Lord honoured his ministry and greatly revived the cause of religion.

On the last day of 1799 Captain Scott suffered another severe affliction when his beloved wife Elizabeth died. They had been married for thirty-one years. Two weeks after her death he wrote to a friend and expressed his wonder at the goodness and faithfulness of God through such a painful trial.

Had not the Lord appeared for us and to us, as our refuge and strength, and very present help in our late, long, and deep affliction and trouble, the floods would have overwhelmed us, and we should have sunk in the mighty waters; but Jehovah is his memorial in all generations. Had I ten thousand tongues, I could not utter the thousandth part of the truth and faithfulness, the goodness and the mercies of the Lord to my dearest earthly treasure in her affliction, and to me his poor, sinful, and worthless worm ... I may say indeed, he made the bed of my dearest in her sickness, and strengthened her by his word and Spirit on her bed of languishing. The Lord never once suffered the Enemy of Souls to take the advantage of her weakness, nor permitted her faith and hope in his word, his faithfulness, and his Christ, utterly to fail.[31]

The pain was still raw on 21 February when he writes in another letter, 'You may conceive something, but very little of what I feel in my present situation, where every object that surrounds me, and especially some things that more particularly claim my attention, remind me afresh continually, and always keep upon my mind my late great loss, open my wound, and make it bleed afresh.'[32] He felt his bereavement deeply, and for a while was desolate and melancholy. But when he saw his beloved no more groaning in her earthly tabernacle, or burdened with sins and diseases, but holy and happy in her Saviour's presence, he ceased to mourn; instead, he gave thanks and glory to God on her account.

He found it almost impossible to pursue his ministerial labours wholeheartedly as his time was now divided between the Lord's work and domestic concerns. This conflict of interests remained until, on 10 June 1802, he married Ann Barrow, the widow of Samuel Barrow, the 'squire' of Nantwich, who had been a friend and protector of the church there. After his marriage he lived and preached alternately at Nantwich and Matlock. During the early part of his ministry he had been accustomed to travel up to twenty miles on the Lord's Day, and to preach five or six times a week, but now in his late sixties he reduced his itinerancy. The Lord in his goodness enabled him to preach until near his death.

The year before he died he witnessed the culmination of much of his work in the founding of the Cheshire Congregational Union at Macclesfield. Several of the churches which he had founded or where he had ministered, such as Nantwich, Congleton, Northwich, Middlewich and Queen Street, Cheshire, were among the founder members. At the second meeting of the Union, held at Nantwich, Scott presented the contribution of the church and William Evans of Stockport preached a sermon appropriately entitled *Encouragements to Exertion in the Spread of the Gospel*. From this point the evangelistic campaigns were less sporadic and more organized, consolidating and expanding the work Scott had begun.

On 12 April 1807 he administered the Lord's Supper at Nantwich for the last time. The occasion was peculiarly blessed to him. He addressed the minister who was to preach on that day with the words, 'O how sweet is the Sabbath Day! May the Lord bless you, my brother, and give you to feel in your heart some of the sweet drops of his love, that you may give it to us warm from the heart!' After the service, he remarked, 'O my poor hard heart! May the Lord soften it! I hope I did feel a little softening today.'[33]

A month later (10 May), at Matlock, he attended public worship for the last time. On the following Friday he became seriously ill and felt his final hours approaching. He lay down and said, 'I am lying down on my dying bed; and I bless God that I am free from either pain or dread.' The next day, in the presence of a servant called Mary, he exclaimed, 'Into your hands, O God, I commit my dear wife and dear friend! Into your hands I commit poor Mary!' He frequently and easily spoke of the blessings that there are in Christ and often cried out, 'Precious Jesus! Precious Jesus! Jesus is precious to me!' On Tuesday 19 May he encouraged a minister to preach the whole gospel, and to keep none of it hidden. 'Use your tongue, brother, for the glory of God. Bring the people to Christ at once, and tell them simply what you know of him, and may the Lord bless you!'[34]

He did not seek pity during his final hours and asked for very little. When his wife inquired if there was anything he wanted, he replied, 'I want nothing but Jesus!' During this time he enjoyed a rare sense of heaven in his heart, which was clearly visible on his countenance. He was deeply humble, too, viewing himself as the chief of sinners. When someone called him 'good sir', he interrupted, 'Don't call me *good*; I wish we may all see more of the poverty and emptiness of the creature, and more of the riches and fulness of the dear Redeemer!' He made the most of every opportunity to help his wife 'give him up to Christ', and to urge the ministers who visited him to preach the gospel. 'Go and tell them,' he told a preacher, who was about to ride into the country to proclaim Christ, 'go and tell them I am going to heaven; but all who die out of Christ will go to hell. Tell them all I am dying and going to heaven!'[35]

On Wednesday 27 May he was very weak and unable to speak. Some of his friends spent some time in prayer for him. He rallied and murmured, 'O tell poor sinners what a sweet and precious Christ I have found, or rather, that has found me.' He was unafraid of dying, because he knew that his Redeemer was alive and ready to welcome him into heaven. On going to bed for the last time, he said, 'Weaker than a bruised reed, help I every moment need!' The Lord did not break the bruised reed, for on the morning of 28 May 1807, he gently carried his child home, without a struggle or groan. His body was interred on 9 June in a vault within the Protestant dissenting chapel in Queen Street, Chester, where his first dear wife was also laid.[36]

George Whitefield described Captain Jonathan Scott as a 'glorious field-officer', while R. Tudur Jones, in *Congregationalism in England*, calls him 'the most pertinacious and successful of itinerant preachers in Lancashire, Shropshire, Staffordshire and particularly Cheshire'.[37] John Fletcher of Madeley was equally impressed. In a letter to Lady Huntingdon, he wrote, 'I went ... to meet Captain Scott ... a captain of the truth—a bold soldier of Jesus Christ. God has thrown down before him the middle wall of bigotry, and he boldly launches into an irregular usefulness ... God keep him zealous and simple! I believe this red coat will shame many a black one. I am sure he shames me.'[38]

Rowland Hill says something similar: 'I knew him a preacher in his red coat before he left the army. Since he has been in the ministry of the word, he has proved himself a labourer that needs not be ashamed, and still continues to bring forth fruit in his old age. Would to God it were my lot to encourage a thousand such soldiers and lay preachers in the same blessed cause.'[39] Henry Venn, writing in 1783, referred to him as 'a bright example of every Christian grace', who 'spends all his strength in preaching to crowded congregations'.[40]

Scott was a strong military character with a warm temper and a genuine religious fervour, which he displayed in both his private and public life. He was wholehearted in his walk with God, upright in his behaviour, and stern and severe in his reproofs. On one occasion, when he was expected to visit a church, one of the members prayed 'that it might please God to bring this brother safely to them, but that he might *leave the rod behind him*'.[41] The depth of his love for Christ and his zeal to spread the gospel never abated. One writer calls him 'an honest, resolute, autocratic man, with a considerable allowance of practical shrewdness, a warm heart and a complete devotion to the cause which he had espoused'.[42]

He was always generous, distributing the money entrusted to him with care and wisdom, and at the same time keeping a close watch over his personal expenditure. It is thought that throughout most of his religious life, after providing for his family, he used the rest of his income for religious and charitable purposes. Before his conversion he complained that he never had enough to supply his wants, whereas after his conversion he enjoyed more than enough although he gave so much away. On 2 October 1786, he wrote to a friend,

Hitherto, my extremities have been God's opportunities. He has suitably, seasonably, and often most marvellously supplied my every want, and helped me through the difficulties of every work he has hitherto condescended to employ me in—having always put it into the hearts of those who were able to help me, when I have needed it. Indeed, through his blessing, my own property has seemed to multiply in using for him … Oh, my dear friend and brother, magnify the Lord with me, and let us exalt his name; for he has done great and marvellous things for us, in us, and by us![43]

He was a sensitive and compassionate man, who found it difficult to endure the death of a bird or an animal, even if it meant food for his family. He cared lovingly for his horse, and always made sure it was well looked after. If he was at the house of a friend, and his animal was neglected, he would change his clothes and thoroughly clean it himself—offering a silent rebuke to his friend's servant—before settling down to eat. Even in his prayers it was common for him to pray for the strength and support of his animal.

Scott had an easy way of bringing Christ into everyday conversations and correspondence. It was not possible to be in his presence for long without hearing something uplifting or edifying. He viewed Christ as superior to every other subject, and nothing and no one, however exalted in the world's eyes, stopped him from introducing him. And yet all was said with such a mixture of good humour and wit that few were offended. It is thought that he never wrote a letter, however far removed the subject of it might be from religious topics, that did not contain some hint or reflection that pointed the reader to Christ.

He was so well respected for his Christianity that rarely did anyone who knew him utter a profanity in his presence. If indecent language was heard by him, it was sure to be reproved. Once a stableman at an inn in Coventry, about to do something for his horse, swore in Scott's hearing. The animal, as if shocked, turned round to look at the servant. Scott, making the most of the opportunity, responded. 'Do you observe how my horse stares at you? He is not used to such bad words at home; he never hears an oath there; and he does not know what to make of it.' Thus the culprit was gently reproved, but not offended.[44]

He was equally adept at giving the thoughtless something serious to think about. On one occasion he met some ladies who came to speak with him after his sermon. 'Do you remember, sir,' one of them said, 'dancing with us at such a time and place?' He replied, 'O yes, madam, I remember it very well; and am much ashamed of those days of my vanity; but madam, you and I are many years older now, and so much nearer death and eternity.' He then proceeded to speak of the great things of God.[45]

Once, after influencing the daughter of a country gentleman by sharing the gospel with her, the enraged father promised to ambush Scott and shoot him. He then challenged him to a duel. Scott boldly called on him and said,

'Sir, I hear you have designed to shoot me—by which you would have been guilty of murder. Failing in this, you have sent me a challenge, and what a coward you must be, sir, to wish to engage with a blind man [Scott was very short-sighted]. As you have given me the challenge, it is now my right to choose the time, the place and the weapon. I appoint the present moment, sir, the place where we now are, and the sword to which I have been most accustomed for the weapon.'

The man was terrified at his words until Scott produced a Bible from his pocket and said, 'This is my sword, sir, the only weapon I will engage with.' When relating this incident to his friends, Scott, with a chuckle, said at this point, 'Never was a poor careless sinner so delighted with the sight of a Bible before.' The father begged Scott's pardon, listened to him and became a firm friend.[46]

Scott was a man of fervent prayer, both in the privacy of his own home and in the pulpit. His sentiments and expressions produced an awful solemnity on his congregations, and highlighted his firm belief in the power and government of God in his own life and in the affairs of the world. His style, it is said, was 'fearless and forcible, somewhat rugged, altogether unadorned'. His sermons, though they could not be admired for their arrangement, or for any particular eloquence or grace in delivery, were mighty in the hands of his Captain, anointed with the power of the Holy Spirit, founded on the doctrines of the Bible, with many pointed appeals to the consciences of men and women. He declared the whole counsel of God without compromise, and when he had experienced the great truths of Scripture in his own heart, as he often did, his sermons were irresistible.

Dugald Macfadyen, who wrote about Scott at the beginning of the twentieth century from one of the churches he had founded, commented,

Whether preaching in a building, or on a horse-block in the open air … Captain Scott was a man who could hardly fail to command the attention of his hearers—mighty in the Scriptures, stern in rebuke, feeling the truth he proclaimed, gracious in urging the offers of the gospel. To his hearers his voice had something of the final trump in it, well suited to rouse sleepers from the death of sin that Christ might shine upon them …

To the last he continued to plead and wrestle, exhort, reprove, command, entreat, in season and out of season, for the salvation of souls. And when men were tired of telling his several virtues, they said he was a Christian gentleman. I do not wonder that they loved him. I cannot even write of him now without feeling my heart warm towards him.[47]

In all, Captain Jonathan Scott was a soldier in the Lord's army. His aim was to rescue sinners from the devil's dominion and lead them into the kingdom of God. To that end he put on the whole armour of God and marched into battle, and to that end he wielded the sword of the Spirit in the name of his commander, Jesus Christ.

Endnotes

1 John Baliol (c.1250–1314) competed with Robert Bruce for the Scottish throne, and Edward I of England decided in his favour. After four years he was deposed by Edward, committed to the Tower, and then banished from the country. He retired to Normandy.

2 **W. Gordon Robinson,** *Jonathan Scott* (London, Independent Press, 1961), p. 4.

3 *Evangelical Magazine*, November 1807, p. 492.

4 This incident may have occurred at a later date.

5 **Henry Venn,** *The Letters of Henry Venn* (Edinburgh, Banner of Truth Trust, 1993 reprint), pp. 535–547.

6 *Evangelical Magazine*, November, 1807, p. 494.

7 **Dugald Macfadyen,** *Transactions of the Congregational Historical Society* (London, 1907–1908), vol. 3, pp. 51–52. Hereafter *TCHS*.

8 *Ibid.,* p. 52.

9 *Evangelical Magazine*, November 1807, p. 495.

10 *TCHS,* p. 53.

11 *Ibid.*

12 *Ibid.*

13 *Evangelical Magazine*, November 1807, p. 494.

14 *Ibid.,* p. 495.

15 A.C.H. Seymour, *The Life and Times of Selina Countess of Huntingdon* (Stoke-on-Trent, Tentmaker, 2000 reprint), vol. 1, p. 406.

16 Luke Tyerman, *The Life of George Whitefield* (London, Hodder & Stoughton, 1877), vol. 2, pp. 502–503.

17 Seymour, *Countess of Huntingdon*, vol. 1, p. 372.

18 *Ibid.,* p. 383.

19 Josiah Bull, *But Now I See: The Life of John Newton* (Edinburgh, Banner of Truth Trust, 1998 reprint), pp. 161–162.

20 *TCHS,* p. 54.

21 Bull, *But Now I See*, p. 166.

22 Tyerman, *Whitefield*, vol. 2, p. 503.

23 Arnold Dallimore, *George Whitefield* (Edinburgh, Banner of Truth Trust, 1970 & 1980), vol. 2, p. 468.

24 *Evangelical Magazine*, December 1807, p. 538.

25 *Ibid.,* pp. 538–539.

26 Venn, *Letters*, p. 238.

27 Robinson, *Jonathan Scott*, p. 8.

28 *TCHS,* p. 58.

29 *Ibid.,* p. 59.

30 *Evangelical Magazine*, December 1807, p. 540.

31 *Ibid.,* p. 541.

32 *Ibid.,* p. 542.

33 *Ibid.,* pp. 542–543.

34 *Ibid.,* p. 543.

35 *Ibid.,* pp. 543–544.

36 *Ibid.,* pp. 544–545.

37 R. Tudur Jones, *Congregationalism in England* (London, Independent Press, 1962), p. 156.

38 Seymour, *Countess of Huntingdon*, vol. 1, p. 406.

39 William Jones, *Memoir of Rowland Hill* (London, Henry G. Bohn, 1853), pp. 56–57.

40 Venn, *Letters*, p. 377.

41 *TCHS,* p. 58.

42 Robinson, *Jonathan Scott,* p. 13.

43 *Evangelical Magazine*, December 1807, p. 546.

44 *Ibid.,* p. 547.

45 *Ibid.*

46 Robinson, *Jonathan Scott,* p. 14.

47 *TCHS,* pp. 49, 66.

David Simpson

The Good Samaritan

(1) Early Years: Preparing for the Fight of Faith

The author of the preface in Simpson's *Key to the Prophecies* speaks of Simpson as 'the greatest and best of men';[1] while Sydney Moore in an article on Simpson's *Hymnbook* in the *Congregational Quarterly*, October 1951, cites what was said of him, 'If all the pulpits in our land were filled with men like Simpson, the devil's dominion would not be worth twelve months' purchase.'[2] Those within the circle of his work and who knew him best as a minister reckoned his 'conduct was an approach to the scriptural description of a *perfect man*'.[3] A pious neighbour and friend, John Whitaker, in a sermon addressed to the Sunday School at Macclesfield in 1799, the year of Simpson's death, said that in 'future years, his name would be pronounced with rapture; that generations then unborn would rise and call him blessed. Posterity,' he added, 'will do justice to his memory, and fame will enrol him in the annals of Macclesfield as its greatest and its worthiest character.'[4] It is hoped that this short memoir will do justice to his memory.

Simpson was born in September 1744 at Ingleby Arncliffe, not far from Northallerton, in Yorkshire, and baptised in the parish church of All Saints on 1 October. In the middle of the eighteenth century the small village of Ingleby had only 58 houses and a population of 253, most of whom in later years did not appreciate Simpson's 'adopted Methodism' and his relationship with the villagers was turbulent at times, although towards the end of his life they supported him more openly. In a letter he wrote in 1795 when revisiting Ingleby, he says, 'Today I am poorly in my head though not confined. In the afternoon I am going, by their desire and particular invitation, to visit a widow lady and her two amiable daughters. They have been prejudiced against me for many years, but appear now to be softening.'[5] A few years later, when he preached for Mr Steel at Ingleby, he wrote, 'The people flocked from all quarters to hear the word and expressed in general much satisfaction. Whether good is done or otherwise, I cannot say, and perhaps it will never be known till the General Audit.'[6]

David Simpson

His parents Anne and Ralph Simpson were highly regarded in the village. Ralph was a small landowner and farm bailiff, who came from a well-known family in the neighbourhood, and Anne was a woman of high morals and kind manners. They had seven children: Anne, who died unmarried in her brother's house in Macclesfield; David; Margaret and Mary, who both lived to marry; Jane, Ralph and a second Jane, who all died in infancy. Ralph senior, although ignorant of evangelical religion, was a 'respectable church-goer of the old Puritan school'.7 He was dignified in his conduct and strictly attentive to the external duties of Christianity. Family worship, a forgotten practice in most households, was not neglected, and was sometimes taken by David. When Ralph died at Hutton Rudby in 1781, leaving his only son residuary legatee on the death of his widow, David felt the loss keenly. He took his mother to live with him in his home at Macclesfield until her death at the age of eighty in 1792. He loved his parents and their passing left a void that was never filled during the last seven years of his life.

Alfred Hunt calls David a 'precocious child … with an active and energetic mind bent especially on history, and a passion for reading. His surroundings appealed to his fertile imagination.'8 It was hoped he would follow in his father's footsteps and become a farmer, but God had other plans. During a time of family worship God spoke to him in a remarkable way, which helped to direct him into the ministry, as David explains:

When I was yet a boy and undesigned for the ministry, either by my parents or from inclination, one Sunday evening, while I was reading prayers in my father's family, suddenly a voice, or something like a voice, called aloud within me, yet so as not to be perceived by any of the persons kneeling around me, 'You must go and be instructed for the ministry.' The voice, or whatever it might be, was so exceedingly quick and powerful, that it was with difficulty I could proceed to the end of the prayer, which was that form for families at the end of the little book called *The Christian Monitor*. As soon, however, as the prayer was ended, I made request to my father to let me be trained up for the ministry; I told him all I knew of the circumstances: he of course denied my request, thinking it was some whim I had got in my head, which would go off again when I had slept upon it. But the voice, or what shall I call it? gave me no rest night or day for three weeks; when my ever dear, honoured, and indulgent father, gave way to my wishes, and put me into a train of study to qualify me for the university.[9]

Simpson's comment about this 'voice from heaven' was simply, 'I pretend not to determine anything about the fact. Only so it was. It produced a very important change in the course of my life. I bless God for it.' There is no doubt that this incident had a profound effect on him, but, according to his own admission, it was not until he was twenty that his mind 'first took a religious turn'.

Simpson's first classical teacher was William Dawson of Northallerton Grammar School, with whom he remained a year. He was then placed under the care of John Noble of Scorton, who was the head of one of the 'most celebrated schools of preparatory education in the neighbourhood'. In the view of Thomas Scott, the famous Bible commentator, who left the school just before Simpson started, Noble 'had been in his time indisputably an able teacher of the learned languages, but at this time he was old and lethargic; and though still assiduous was most grossly imposed upon by the boys'.[10] Noble, however, did take a keen interest in Simpson, who stayed there two years, and imbibed 'a love for the Classics of Greece and Rome'. He also noted the 'pernicious effect reading and translating into English verse the beautiful songs of Anacreon, in praise of Bacchus and Venus' had on his mind.

On 10 June 1765 he entered St John's College in Cambridge University, where he studied for about three years. One of his favourite pastimes was reading in the 'fair and beautiful library' of the university, as Simpson calls it. He soon wrote to his former master John Noble, who replied on 17 October 1765:

St John's College, Cambridge, where Simpson was converted

I had yours and am glad to hear you approve of your present

situation. St John's is a college where a young man has a fine opportunity to improve, if study be his object …

I hope you will continue the same application you used at Scorton, and a regular deportment under the many temptations to which you must inevitably be exposed. This will be remarked by the master and fellows and will turn to your advantage whether you succeed to a fellowship, or go out to a curacy. I am glad you have got a scholarship, which will be some alleviation of your expenses.

You, I find, remember what I recommended to you in respect of sequestering some part of your time from your academical studies to that of divinity, which may easily be done without any detriment to the former, if only Saturdays and Sundays be employed in reading some few books that may be preparative to a more close study of divinity.[11]

Noble then lists a number of books on divinity and ecclesiastical history for Simpson's perusal.

He had a good grounding at the university, and in June 1766 it was noted that he had done 'well in logic and algebra, but had neglected the Greek'. Up until his conversion his general conduct and literary attainments were both applauded by his tutor; but after his conversion his progress in knowledge was less noticeable, and he was exposed to the censure of his superiors and the sarcasm of his fellow students. While at Cambridge the thorny question of whether the undergraduates should be compelled to subscribe to the Thirty-Nine Articles was being discussed. His views as a young man are not known, but just before his death, he wrote with obvious feeling, 'Can anything in the whole absurd systems of Popery be more improper than to make every young man without exception subscribe … How is it likely that a boy, raw from school, should be competent to such a task? And if he is to subscribe upon the faith of others, on the same principle he may subscribe to the Mass Book, the Koran, or any other book whatever.'[12] Simpson took his BA degree in 1769 and obtained a third class, and his MA in 1772.

On his first vacation from Cambridge (June 1766) he returned to his father's house, where he received an invitation from Theophilus Lindsey, then resident in his vicarage of Catterick in Yorkshire and later an able defender of the doctrines of Socinus, to spend some time with him at his house. During the course of their conversation, Lindsey carefully examined Simpson on the nature of his studies and the use he made of his time. Lindsey was surprised to discover that Simpson had not been studying the Scriptures, although they were to be the foundation of his ministry. He strongly admonished his guest for such inexcusable neglect and urged him to read and study the Bible.

This rebuke and the good effect it had on Simpson helped to build a lasting relationship between the two men. Simpson called his friend 'the amiable Mr Lindsey, to whom I am under great obligations', and when coupling him with Joseph Priestley, referred to them as 'the men I love; their religious opinions I detest; in our morality we are agreed; in our divinity we differ'.[13]

The absence of a Bible was certainly not uncommon, and Simpson himself, while at Cambridge, knew men who attained to the highest honours without ever having a Bible in their rooms, unless occasionally borrowed, for the whole four years! Edward Parsons, in referring to Simpson's conversation with Lindsey, comments:

Theophilus Lindsey, who urged Simpson to read and study the Scriptures. They became good friends.

From this conversation at the vicarage of Catterick, we date the decisive revolution that took place in his sentiments and feelings, and which determined the character of his future studies, and issued in a life of eminent usefulness to the cause of evangelical religion. The expostulations of his friend came with effectual power to his mind. He felt the criminality of his former indifference and inattention to the divine writings, and was filled with corresponding remorse. The awful concerns of eternity so powerfully impressed his mind, that all other concerns dwindled into insignificance, and were almost wholly forgotten.[14]

It is true that Simpson was deeply ashamed that he did not have a Bible in his library and immediately acquired a quarto Bible with marginal references. It is also true that he began to study it diligently; but Parsons overstates his case when he imagines that 'from this time biblical knowledge became the supreme object of his ambition and delight', for on his return to university he was embarrassed at the thought of the Bible being found on his desk, afraid that his companions might brand him a 'Methodist'.

Soon after his encounter with Lindsey, he received further 'encouragement' to read the Bible when, on his way back to Cambridge, he was stopped by a highwayman, who pointed a pistol at him and demanded money. The question 'Am I ready to die?' flashed into his mind, his conscience immediately replying 'No!' On his return to university he was deeply moved by a letter from Thomas Joy, informing him of John Noble's death: 'I saw him when his last hour was fast approaching; he was very sensible; received me as he always did, with kind affection; was thankful for my visit; *and named you with tenderness* ... The funeral was truly solemn. I could perceive tears stealing down the cheeks of many.'[15] Noble was buried in Bolton Church. On his monument he is described as 'a man of primitive simplicity and faith; a true Christian priest; a most sweet friend, the best of patrons; a learned, faithful and pious teacher'. These events, highlighting the fragility of life, spurred Simpson on to examine the word of God more closely.

His relationship with Rowland Hill, a student at the same college, also proved a major influence in directing his life. Hill, whom Simpson first met in April 1767, was on the lookout for like-minded individuals, so when he noticed Simpson's strict morality and seriousness, he introduced himself and the two men became good friends; they read together in the Greek New Testament and evangelical publications, and always concluded their meetings with prayer.

Rowland Hill, one of Simpson's life-long friends

Their friendship lasted for the rest of their lives. When Hill preached in the neighbourhood of Cambridge, and visited jails, workhouses and sick rooms, calling sinners to repentance, Simpson was one of the men who accompanied him, although it seems he did not preach.

Later in life Simpson frequently urged his friend to preach in his new church at Macclesfield, which on one occasion solicited the following response, 'It grieves me that I fear it will not be in my power to visit Macclesfield according to the affectionate wishes of my heart. London engagements much circumscribe my country excursions. However, when I *can* come to see you I will; but when that will be, I dare not promise.'[16] Hill eventually travelled to Macclesfield and occupied Simpson's pulpit. On one of these visits, as late as 1798, he said, 'My very affectionate old friend was anxious that I should preach to the people of his charge; though it was not the regular evening for the lecture. His large church presented a very serious and crowded congregation, to whom I attempted to explain the mind that was in Christ Jesus, and its consequent effects on the Christian, from Philippians 2:5.'[17] He noted in his journal, 'A visit to this town (Macclesfield) was a peculiar pleasure and satisfaction to my mind. Mr Simpson, the minister of the new church, is my dear old friend. Our acquaintance commenced at Cambridge.'[18]

At Cambridge, Hill introduced Simpson to a society of devout collegians, among whom were Thomas Pentycross and Charles de Coetlogon, and they supported one another through difficult times. In the journal of his first tour in Scotland, Hill looked back to those 'dark' days and the reaction of other students to their faith.

The university was *then* almost in total darkness. No wonder, therefore, if for such exercises, and for some other strong symptoms of a methodistical bias, we were speedily marked, and had the honour of being pointed at, as the curiosities of the day. This did good: others joined us, to the number of ten or twelve. Some of them were Nicodemian disciples: others have proved bold and useful ministers, and some of them, I trust, have been taken to glory.[19]

It was partly through the influence of this group that Simpson was eventually converted. It is not possible to put an exact date on his rebirth, but it was during his time at Cambridge, probably in 1767. Many years later in a sermon on Psalm 126:5—while encouraging his congregation to 'seek the Lord in simplicity and sincerity', and to expect to find him 'every day, every hour, every moment, under every sermon, under every chapter, under every prayer, under every ordinance; yea, every hour of the day, when your hands are employed in your daily calling'—he recalled his own salvation. 'I well remember, when it first pleased God to visit my own soul with this spiritual and evangelical deliverance, I was sitting at breakfast in my own room at Cambridge.'[20] A new sense of his own wretchedness was powerfully wrought in his heart. 'He mourned, he wept, and prayed.' One day, probably soon after his 'deliverance', being in prayer, 'he had such a view of his past sinfulness and present guilt and pollution, as almost deprived him of hope. But the Lord suddenly removed his burden, and whispered peace and pardon to his soul. He felt his sins were all forgiven. He renounced the pomps and vanities of the world.'[21]

'This was an era in his Christian experience,' comments Gaulter, 'the recollection of which, no variety of circumstances could enfeeble or erase. He cherished the remembrance with an ardour of feeling, and gratitude to the *God of all grace*, not exceeded in the records of Christianity.'[22] From this time he never hesitated to say, with great confidence, that '*then* God revealed to him his mercy in Christ Jesus, and satisfied him of his *pardon and acceptance*. His heart glowed with love to the Redeemer, and the song of joy and deliverance was upon his lips. There is reason to believe that he continued to walk in the light of this heavenly consolation until the end of his mortal journey.'[23]

Before his conversion the branch of learning that interested him most was mathematical science, and there is no reason to doubt that he would have achieved eminence in that sphere. But after his conversion mathematics quickly gave way to the study of theology as he prepared himself for the ministry. He pored over the Bible, hungry to know his Saviour more and the truths he taught. In a glowing recommendation of the book he had once neglected, he wrote:

If a book was professedly to come from God, to teach mankind his will, what should we expect its contents to be? Should we expect to be told the nature and perfections of

God? The nature and perfections of God are in the Bible alone made known. Should we expect to know how all things came into being at first? The Bible alone declares it. Should we wish to know what the Lord God requires of his creatures? This the Bible makes known—*supreme love*. Should we want to know the reward of obedience? The Bible points out eternal joys. Would curiosity lead us to inquire the reward of disobedience? The Bible reveals extreme, everlasting misery. Should we inquire what is our duty to each other? In the Bible it is written, as with a sunbeam—love all men as yourselves. Would we know the original of those miseries and disorders, which we observe in the world? and how a merciful God can permit them? The Bible points to the cause and proclaims death and every evil to be the wages of sin. Would we know whence are those strange disorders we each of us feel in our own natures? The Bible informs us we are all in a state of ruin—we are *fallen* creatures. Would we discover how sin is pardoned, our natures restored, and God's perfections glorified? Though this was hid from ages and generations of the heathen, the Bible makes it as clear as the sun—by the death of Christ and the operations of the Spirit. What could we require in a book from God that is *not* to be found in the Bible?[24]

While at Cambridge, Simpson became acquainted with Robert Robinson, the pastor of a Baptist congregation in the town. Robinson was a scholarly and eloquent preacher, whose doctrines were initially evangelical. Simpson became very friendly with him, and received great benefit from his instruction, often repeating a well chosen comment he received from him subsequent to his ordination, 'Now, young man, you must cry a *sale of character*,' which proved sound advice in view of the problems he would encounter in his ministry. After he left Cambridge the two men corresponded for some time. Sadly, Robinson turned his back on conservative theology and became a proselyte of the Socinian Joseph Priestley.

Although Simpson became impatient and desired to preach the gospel as soon as possible, he did not join Hill and the others in 'field preaching' or adopt other 'irregular practices' at this time. This is confirmed by a student at the university, who was not shackled, like Simpson, by ecclesiastical order and 'correctness'. 'You need not, I think, mention anything to Simpson of what I design by the help of God to do in the ministry, either now or afterwards. I dare not give him any pain; and though we think differently about the methods of advancing the kingdom of Christ, yet I am sure his eye is more single than mine, and what I very often think in myself to be burning zeal is nothing but constitution.'[25]

Despite his early scruples, Simpson recognised the importance of preaching to the lost, and often bemoaned the sparsity of good gospel men. In a letter he wrote in 1798, he remarks, 'All over this country, with a few exceptions, the people seem to be sitting in the region and shadow of death, in every religious sense, none to take them by the hand and lead them into the way of peace.'[26]

In his eagerness to preach he hurried to his Cambridge tutor and earnestly requested that he be allowed to take his degree not in divinity but in law, which was a shorter course, so he could be ordained more quickly. His tutor, guided by the silent hand of providence, declined his request and Simpson continued his divinity studies. After his degree he left the university and spent the next eight months in quiet study at home.

Simpson left university with many good friends, among whom were Francis Blackburne and John Jebb, both of whom had been introduced to him by Lindsey. Joseph Milner and William Paley, a fellow Yorkshireman and a close friend of William Unwin, who had been Simpson's senior fellow student at college, were two other acquaintances. Simpson quotes Paley with approval and earnestly commends his *Evidences*. 'I admire the abilities of the man.' Many others were influenced for good by Simpson's behaviour at university. Years after, Thomas Robinson, a young fellow of Trinity, bore testimony 'to the strength given him by the observation of his consistent life'.

On 24 September 1769, Simpson was ordained deacon at St Paul's Cathedral by Richard Terrick, bishop of London. (He was ordained priest in 1771.) In October he settled at All Saints Church as curate to his friend William Unwin of Stock Harward, which

Mary Unwin, the mother of William Unwin of Stock Harward

was united with Ramsden Bellhouse in Essex, where he enjoyed an agreeable two years. Unwin did all he could to help his new curate and the two men enjoyed rich fellowship. During his stay he became friendly with Unwin's mother, Mary, whom he had first met at Cambridge, when she came to nurse her seriously sick son. Later in life he stayed with her and the poet William Cowper at Olney.

The famous poet William Cowper, with whom Simpson stayed in later life

From the outset Simpson was held in great affection by his parishioners and they responded positively to his ministry, although many struggled with drunkenness. Simpson speaks of a parishioner who was so intoxicated that he fell into the river and drowned, while the register of Stock and Ramsden Bellhouse notes that another 'drunken, passionate, poor, an object of pity, departed', a miserable end to a miserable life. Indeed, when Simpson arrived at Stock, the parish was described as 'profligate to a proverb, in a state of the most notorious depravity'; but during the short time he was there, he assisted in the beginnings of a reformation. It was therefore a surprise and disappointment to his parishioners when he decided to move to Buckingham, a decision that not even Simpson fully understood.

He settled in Buckingham under the sanction of John Newton and Charles de Coetlogon as curate to Thomas Price, an old man in poor health, who deputed most of the preaching to him. However, the inhabitants of the town received him without reverence or honour, and reacted antagonistically to his sermons, which he had previously preached at Stock without causing offence. Soon, on account of his enthusiastic preaching of the doctrines of justification by faith and the nature and necessity of the new birth, and his insistence on a personal application of the truths of the Bible to the consciences of his hearers, there was a concerted effort to remove him from office. An appeal was made to his diocesan to withdraw his licence. John Newton, who was watching developments, wrote in his diary for 27 April 1772, 'Attended the Archdeacon's visitation at Stratford—a poor, uncomfortable service. Heard a sermon in the usual strain from Romans 1:22. Met Mr Simpson, who is likely to be forced from Buckingham. The poor people who have willingly received the gospel are much to be pitied.'[27] Bishop Green, a forthright opponent of Methodism, after hearing the charges against him, withdrew his licence and then said, 'Mr Simpson, if you are determined to do your duty, as a clergyman ought to do, you must everywhere expect to meet with opposition.'[28]

The hostility he met with at Buckingham was compensated by the fact that large numbers attended his preaching and several were converted under his ministry. In a letter written sixty years later, the author mentions three converts—his own mother, an old lady he visited when a boy, and a third woman who with tears of joy acknowledged that her conversion was due to Simpson. John West, a farm labourer, was greatly impressed with Simpson's earnestness as a preacher and after Simpson had left Buckingham, the recollection of his sermons was used by God to bring him to a personal knowledge of salvation. He later became a wealthy man, started a Sunday School in Gawcott, a hamlet about a mile and a half from the town, and spent at least £5000 of his own money building a church there. Thomas Scott, the younger son of the Bible commentator, became the first perpetual curate of Gawcott Chapel.

The Goode family were also singularly blessed by his ministry. After Simpson had left Buckingham, the father wrote to him:

Oh, that we could once more see you among us, as our shepherd; how it would gladden the hearts of our people here; indeed, our house appears as if we had lately buried somebody ... Mr Price's death was about a fortnight ago ... Oh, how heartily we wish we had you with us now ... Your kind concern for the eternal welfare of myself and family I know not how to acknowledge enough ... This visible alteration in many here, particularly my own family, we attribute, under God, to the blessing of having you with us that short time.[29]

The effect of Simpson's ministry is confirmed by William Goode, William

Romaine's successor at St Andrew by the Wardrobe and St Ann's, Blackfriars: 'In attendance on his ministry, my father's mind was more than ordinarily impressed with the sense of the nature and importance of personal religion. To this gentleman's ministrations I have frequently heard my father attribute his first clear and decisive convictions of the great importance of personal religion.'[30] William's brother John, wrote to Simpson and said, 'My sisters and I have always looked upon you as our spiritual father.' He went on to detail the benefit he had 'received from his preaching and prayers' and the obligations he felt to give thanks to God for him. He added, 'Alas! where was I wandering, when the Lord sent you among us? Where, but in the wilderness of this world; lost to all care and concern about God, and Christ, and salvation.'[31]

Many years later, the second Mrs Simpson, in a letter to her daughter, wrote, 'Yesterday your father told me he had heard good news. Mr Ryle told him that he had heard in a bookseller's shop in London some conversation—your dear father the subject—how he had been the honoured instrument of the conversion of two eminent ministers: one in the Church, the other a dissenting minister. This encouraged him.'[32] The dissenting minister was of course John Goode of White Row, Spitalfields.

When he was about to leave Buckingham, a parishioner who had been converted under his ministry, fearing that his successor 'knew not God', asked his advice. Apparently, without hesitation, he replied, 'Join the dissenters,' knowing that the gospel was preached at their meeting house. Accordingly, after his departure several left the Church for the dissenters and a general indifference pervaded the parish. Others were confused and thought Simpson wanted them to stay in the Church of England. In one letter the writer asks whether it was true that Simpson had urged everyone who valued his teaching to *stay within the Church*. This led many, who wanted to worship elsewhere, to remain *in the Church*. Interestingly, after he had left, even his opponents were less antagonistic towards him. 'I have never heard one disrespectful word of you since you left,' wrote a parishioner. 'Even your enemies are more favourable in what they say than when you were here.'[33]

While Unwin was at Tunbridge Wells with Lady Huntingdon he mentioned Simpson to her as a man suitable to take charge of her chapel in the town, and offered to be the bearer of any proposals, which she might make to that effect. Unfortunately for the countess the offer came just too late, for two days earlier Simpson had agreed to move to Macclesfield. When Unwin told her the news, she 'much regretted this engagement of his friend, as she appears to have anticipated much utility to the cause of God by his becoming minister of the chapel at Tunbridge Wells, and superintendent of the work throughout the county of Kent'.[34] After Simpson's second suspension, Lady Huntingdon repeated the offer, but it was again refused.

Charles Roe, who invited Simpson to Macclesfield

It may well have been the problems he experienced at Buckingham that encouraged him to accept the invitation of a leading entrepreneur Charles Roe to his residence in Macclesfield. Apparently, the invitation came through an association with a relative of Roe's wife, Rachel Harriot. Little is known about Mrs Roe, but on 19 July 1764, John Wesley rode to Macclesfield, where he 'heard an agreeable account' of her. He wrote in his *Journal:*

[She] was in the society at London from a child; but after she was married to a rich man [Charles Roe], durst not own a poor, despised people. Last year she broke through, and came to see me. A few words which I then spoke never left her, not even in the trying hour, during the illness which came a few months after. All her conversation was then in heaven; till feeling her strength was quite exhausted, she said, with a smile, 'death, thou art welcome!' and resigned her spirit.[35]

Obverse of a Roe & Co. halfpenny of 1789, around which is the legend: 'CHARLES ROE ESTABLISHED THE COPPER WORKS 1758', a reference to the Macclesfield copper works

Her husband Charles, the youngest son of Thomas Roe, the vicar of Castleton in Derbyshire, erected the first silk mill in Macclesfield in 1744 and was involved in the production of brass and then copper. It was owing to his influence that Macclesfield expanded so rapidly in the third quarter of the eighteenth century, from an old market town into an industrial centre. Roe not only wanted to meet Simpson, about whom he had heard glowing reports, but to introduce him to Macclesfield and to the prime curate of St Michael's, John Burscoe. The meeting obviously went well as Burscoe, the chapel wardens and several principal inhabitants of the town nominated Simpson for the vacancy at the church. The bishop of Chester accepted the nomination and duly appointed him assistant curate of St

St Michael's, Macclesfield, where Simpson was appointed assistant curate in 1772 (this is not the St Michael's of the 18th century, but a very late Victorian re-build)

Michael's, the only church in the town, on 1 June 1772, the licence simply reading, 'David Simpson of Buckingham, clerk.' Little did the new curate know at the time the battles that lay ahead and the victory that God was ultimately going to grant him.

(2) Macclesfield: The Battle Rages

John Corry in *The History of Macclesfield* speaks in adulatory terms when he describes Simpson as

… one of the most extraordinary and useful men that ever resided in Macclesfield; a man whose knowledge was conducive to the improvement of thousands who were remarkable for their ignorance and sensuality when he first came hither, and whose piety and benevolence gradually prevailed over the prejudices and passions of a large majority of this community … [He was] a man who fearlessly reproved the vicious, overawed the profane, instructed the ignorant, and enlightened the dark and degenerate mind with the renovating irradiations imparted to him by the Sun of Righteousness.[1]

It is certainly true that Simpson's forthright stand for gospel righteousness helped to change the vulgar and sensual behaviour of many in the town.

He also found at Macclesfield 'a most pleasant colleague' in the prime curate John Burscoe, who allowed him to preach the gospel with a fervour that soon awakened the antagonism of his enemies. In and out of the pulpit he attacked sin in all its heinous

'View of Macclesfield' from an engraving published 7 June 1794 by I Stockdale, Piccadilly

and deceptive forms, and enforced the doctrines of forgiveness through faith in the blood of Christ and the fruit and witness of the Spirit. Many were convinced of the truth and converted, while others, who could not endure evangelical truth, strongly resisted his message and spread an unfavourable report of 'this vile Methodist'.

It was a severe trial to Simpson when Burscoe died in February 1773. While waiting for the appointment of a successor, he was in sole but temporary charge and preached to crowded congregations. It was therefore a disappointment when he was nominated to the vacant post by the mayor James Rowson, who had the disposal of it, only for the bishop of Chester to insist on having his own candidate, Thomas Hewson, ordained. Before long friction ensued between the two men. Simpson was a popular and gifted curate, who rightly expected an equal share of the preaching, as had been the custom for many years, but Hewson objected, claiming and exercising the right to preach as often as he wanted, to the exclusion of Simpson. Many in the congregation took offence at Hewson's provocative action, and with anonymous newspaper letters, a party spirit was inflamed. In order to settle the matter, a leading member of the congregation invited both men to his house for a 'peace meeting', in which Hewson was forced to re-establish the customary division of duty, and a fragile truce agreed.

Towards the end of the year, however, Simpson was asked to preach a 'club sermon', a request that greatly annoyed Hewson, who, in retaliation, refused to allow Simpson to take any part in either of the services on 26 December. He repeated this restriction on the afternoon of the following Sunday, which so incensed many of the congregation that they followed Hewson to his own door expressing their resentment. Soon the whole town was in a state of excitement and a parochial meeting was called to consider the best way forward. Once again peace was restored, but only for a season.

It could not help being noticed that many more people attended the church when it was Simpson's turn to preach, which rankled Hewson and his supporters; but this is hardly surprising as the contrast between the two preachers was remarkable. Simpson, with pathos and zeal, earnestly persuaded his hearers to turn to Christ for salvation and to reject the delusions of the world; whereas Hewson, with a cold formality, delivered his moral lessons without reference to the power and life of true godliness.

After a while Simpson could not stand Hewson's 'essays of death' any longer, and decided to expose publicly this abuse of preaching. Accordingly, when asked to preach a charity sermon, he ascended the pulpit in the afternoon as usual and started to preach from exactly the same text as the prime curate had chosen in the morning. In contrast to the dry and liberal 'readings' of Hewson, Simpson spoke with an evangelical passion that gripped the attention of his hearers. He had not been preaching long, when the prime curate, realising what Simpson was doing, jumped out of his seat, marched into the pulpit and, forgetting all decorum, grabbed his fellow curate by the neck and threw him to the ground. Naturally this caused considerable agitation, and before long the church was in an uproar, with many taking sides. Charles Roe then stood up and shouted out that he was a friend of Simpson's and that if that church was denied him, he would build him one himself.

No doubt spurred on by this incident, Robert Roe, Charles's youngest son, bitterly opposed Simpson and wrote in unmeasured terms to his cousin, Hester Ann Roe, the daughter of Rev. James Roe, Charles's brother and a former minister of the parish church. Influenced by Robert's rantings, Hester expressed a view, which serves as a good example of the opinion held by many of his adversaries.

In the summer of 1773, when at Adlington, I heard various accounts of a clergyman whom my uncle Roe had recommended to be curate at Macclesfield, and who was said to be a Methodist. This conveyed to my mind as unpleasant an idea of him as if he had been called a Romish priest; being fully persuaded that to be a Methodist was to be all that is vile under the mask of piety … I heard also that this new clergyman preached against all my favourite diversions, such as going to plays, reading novels, attending balls, assemblies, card tables, &c. But I resolved he should not make a convert of *me*; and that if I found him such as was represented, I would not go often to hear him.

When I returned to Macclesfield, the whole town was in an alarm. My uncle Roe and my cousins [with the exception of Robert] seemed very fond of Mr Simpson, and told me he was a most excellent man; but all the rest of my relations were exasperated against him.[2]

However, the Lord honoured his ministry, and many of his former enemies became his friends. Even Hester Ann, as a teenager, began to consider the objections Simpson urged against dancing, which 'brought powerful convictions' to her mind, although she desired to resist them. As time went by, Simpson's sermons began to sink deeply into her heart and she often came out of church weeping. At the beginning of the following year she was struck by a sermon he preached on, 'What is a man profited, if he shall gain the whole world and lose his own soul?' The impression was deepened by his discourse on the church at Laodicea, and after he had preached on John 3:3, she wrote, 'While Mr Simpson preached on the new birth … I saw and felt, as I had never done before, that I must experience that divine change or perish.'

On the Sunday before Easter she listened eagerly to a sermon in which Simpson described his own conversion.

Lord [she said], if this is truth (and I cannot disbelieve it), never let me rest till I obtain a like blessing … When in the application of his sermon, he asked, 'Now what think you of the state of your souls before God?' I felt myself indeed a lost, perishing, undone sinner; a rebel against repeated convictions and drawings; a rebel against light and knowledge; a condemned criminal by the law of God, who deserved to be sentenced to eternal pain. I wept aloud, so that all around me were amazed, nor did I any longer feel ashamed to own the cause. I went home, ran upstairs, and fell on my knees, and made a

solemn vow to renounce and forsake all my sinful pleasures and trifling companions …
I could do nothing now but bewail my own sinfulness, and cry for mercy. Thus I
continued till Good Friday. My mother thought I was losing my senses, and all my
friends endeavoured to comfort me in vain. After many conflicts and strong fears, I
ventured, however, once more to approach the Lord's Table. As Mr Simpson was
reading that sentence in the Communion Service, 'If any man sin, we have an advocate
with the Father, Jesus Christ the righteous; and he is the propitiation for our sins,' a ray
of divine light and comfort was darted on my soul, and I cried, 'Lord Jesus, let me feel
thou art the propitiation for *my* sins.' I was enabled to believe there was mercy for me;
and I, even I, should be saved![3]

After her conversion she began to attend Methodist meetings despite fierce
opposition from her family, and became a regular correspondent of John
Wesley, who appointed her a class leader in 1781. She married the Wesleyan
itinerant James Rogers in 1784 and soon the couple moved to Dublin, where
Hester helped her husband in his ministry to such an extent that he claimed
2000 were converted through her influence. By 1790 her health began to fail
and so James was moved to City Road Chapel in London, where Hester
became Wesley's housekeeper and was by his bedside when the great
preacher died the following year.

Robert Roe had several interviews with Simpson in which he forcefully
and somewhat rudely expressed his opposition to the curate's preaching,
but each time Simpson responded with kindness and courtesy, thereby
making a good impression on the young assailant. Robert then received a
letter from Hester detailing her own conversion. Outwardly he made a
show of being appalled at her capitulation, but in his heart he knew she was
right, though he dared not admit it. The turning point came on Sunday 22
October 1775 in Roe's drawing room. Simpson's sermon on that day deeply
affected him and that night he said to his father, 'I am sure God was with us
this morning.' Robert again spoke to Simpson, but this time with a humble
and submissive attitude. Soon he started to attend the Methodist meetings
and subsequently joined the society.

Perhaps surprisingly, Charles Roe was vehemently opposed to the
Methodists and demanded a promise from Robert that he would not attend
any more of their meetings, a promise that Robert would not give. To make

matters worse two of his other children followed Robert's example. Charles retaliated by stating that he would cut out of his will any son of his who became a Methodist. One immediately left home, another submitted to his demands, while Robert refused to comply; so Charles barred him from his house. This left Simpson in a difficult position. Having been the means of Robert's conversion and a keen supporter of Methodism, he had every sympathy with the young man, but he also saw the need for children to 'obey their parents'. Thus he threw his support behind Charles, although he remained on friendly terms with Robert, who became an effective preacher of the gospel.

Thankfully, a reconciliation took place before Charles died. In his last illness he spoke to Simpson on many occasions, and with his friend's support and wise counsel, managed to forgive his children. He also earnestly prayed for his own forgiveness and though extremely weak insisted on kneeling up in bed as a mark of genuine repentance.

Simpson had not been at Macclesfield long when he met and fell in love with Ann Waldy of Yarm, a young lady of 'distinguished excellence and piety'. They decided to marry, but their wedding had to be postponed because Simpson was struck by a severe illness. He was nursed back to health by Mrs Roe, who invited Ann to live with her until their own house was ready. In a letter, Mrs Roe said, 'I am of opinion that a lady of Miss Waldy's happy turn of mind, who, like Mary, has chosen the better part, will stand as good a chance of happiness with him as any person on earth … I often tell my Friend that I wish he had a good wife to take care of him.'[4] In one of Ann's letters to her fiancé, she wisely wanted to sort out any slight differences that might exist between them before they were married.

Pray do tell me what it is you disapprove in the genteeler women among the Methodists? When at Yarm I might be mistaken, but could not help thinking you entertain'd some little prejudice against them, which I assure you, has often caused me uneasiness. I could not forbear anticipating some future unhappiness, consequent on my attachment to the Methodists [Ann was a member of Yarm Methodist Society]—which I hope will ever continue, should I ever be united to Mr Simpson if he was not likeminded. But from what you have said I trust this is not the case.[5]

They were eventually married at Yarm on 27 May 1773. For several months the newly-weds lived with the Roes until they moved into their own house in September. Sadly, fifteen months after their union, Ann died on 16 September 1774. She was only twenty-four. As she lay in her husband's arms, her last words to her attendants were, 'Seek the Lord. He is a glorious God. He is a gracious God; and if you seek him, he will be found of you.'[6] She made a favourable and lasting impression on Roe's two daughters, Mary and Frances, who never forgot their conversation with her two days before her death, when she exhorted them to 'labour earnestly for an interest in Christ, and not to set their affections on pleasures, or anything in this world, as they could never afford any real comfort and satisfaction in the prospect of death'.[7] She left David a baby girl, Ann, who married John Lee, a reputable attorney of Wem in Shropshire.

For a while Simpson was distraught and it was only the hope of eternity that pulled him through. He always spoke of his wife with the highest affection and never ceased to cherish her memory. Part of her epitaph reads, 'As a woman, her form was elegant, her manners gentle; as a wife, she was kind, affectionate, obedient; as a Christian, she counted all things but loss, for the excellency of the knowledge of Christ Jesus our Lord. And deeply convinced that professions without practice are vain, she denied ungodliness and worldly lusts, and lived soberly, righteously and godly in this present world.'[8]

On Easter Day 1774 John Wesley rode into Macclesfield and probably for the first time met Simpson. It was the beginning of a long and fruitful friendship, not only with Wesley, but with the Methodists, whom he welcomed to his church and in return often visited their chapel on Sunday evenings. 'The church was usually filled to overflowing and numbered many hundreds at her communion table … Two great bodies, each preserving its own distinctive character, and yet blending in social worship, alternatively at church and chapel.'[9] His support for the Methodists is demonstrated in a sermon he preached on Sunday 22 February 1784 from Psalm 116:5 entitled *The Happiness of Dying in the Lord*. It was occasioned by the death of Martha Rogers, the first wife of James Rogers, a preacher in Wesley's societies, who in the same year married Hester Ann Roe, and contained 'an apology for the Methodists'.

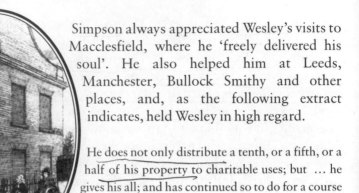

Simpson always appreciated Wesley's visits to Macclesfield, where he 'freely delivered his soul'. He also helped him at Leeds, Manchester, Bullock Smithy and other places, and, as the following extract indicates, held Wesley in high regard.

He does not only distribute a tenth, or a fifth, or a half of his property to charitable uses; but ... he gives his all; and has continued so to do for a course of many years. If to this be added ... that he has been instrumental in the hands of providence in reclaiming more wicked and abandoned persons from the error of their ways than any other man living, and making them sober, steady, useful members of society; so that from being poor, ignorant, and abandoned, they are become opulent, regular in their deportment, and valuable members of the community, (which, I believe, is granted by his most implacable adversaries)—then it will follow, that this despised veteran must be considered as the greatest benefactor to mankind in England, perhaps in the world.[10]

An imaginary sketch of David Simpson meeting John Wesley on the doorstep of Park Green Parsonage before they went to Christ Church

In return Wesley described Simpson as 'an agreeable man' and welcomed him to his conferences.

During the early years of his Christian pilgrimage Simpson was a committed if mild Calvinist. In his own words, he said, 'When my mind took a religious turn, which was not until I was upwards of twenty years of age, I accidentally met with the Bishops' Bible, from the notes of which I embraced the doctrines of Calvinism, and continued both to believe and practise them for several years, but in moderation.'[11] But after his friendship with Wesley and through the influence of his wife, he broke with the past and followed the more liberal tenets of Methodism. In fact, later in life he regarded Calvinism as offensive and stated publicly that nothing would again induce him to subscribe to the Articles and Liturgy. His objections in this area were probably fuelled by Augustus Toplady, whose preaching he found disagreeable, and may have been one of the main reasons why he eventually decided to leave the Church of England.

In the same year as Wesley's visit, Simpson preached a sermon on marriage, entitled *Marriage Honourable, Whoredom Damnable*, in which he stated in no uncertain terms that

... all who indulge to the gratification of their carnal inclinations, in any other way, than that of legal matrimony, are guilty of uncleanness, adultery, or fornication. And we are assured in the most solemn, serious, and positive manner, in different parts of the word of God, that none such have any share, or inheritance, in the kingdom of Christ and of God ...

Next time then, O sinner, next time you are guilty of any criminal indulgence; next time, and every time you commit the unclean act; next time you pollute your body, or defile your lips with foolish, impure, unchristian, unmanly conversation ... remember, O remember, that the drawn sword of divine justice is suspended over your guilty head. Remember, that you are selling your all, your eternal all—for what? The gratification of a vile lust. Remember that you are plunging yourself in endless misery and ruin—for what? Alas, for what! 'Tis a shame even to mention what!

Repent like David—weep like Peter—love like Magdalene—live like the Redeemer of the world. But if instead of this you harden your neck, persist in your unclean courses, and live in contempt both of divine and human laws, your case is desperate. You will live pitied and despised by the virtuous and the good. You will die in disgrace. You will rise in shame. You will be struck with tenfold confusion before the bar of God.[12]

This sermon deeply offended a wealthy, influential and adulterous businessman, Sir William Meredith of Henbury Hall, who was vociferous in his hostility. Those who had opposed Simpson at first were now encouraged by their new ally to do everything they could to silence 'the offender', trumpeting up a charge of 'Methodism'. They censured his preaching, reviled his character and appealed to his diocesan, the bishop of Chester, William Markham, who, because of an inherent fear of Methodism and its apparent dangers, suspended him in the autumn of 1774, angrily observing that 'to *him* the Methodists owed all their success in Macclesfield'. 'My Lord,' replied Simpson calmly, 'I cannot take that honour to myself.' 'Thus,' remarks John Gaulter, 'he was twice suspended for teaching, according to a creed to which he was sworn and had subscribed, when deviation would have been a flagrant violation of the most sacred oaths.'[13]

It is worth noting, in connection with the opposition he endured, that a sermon he published in 1774 on *The Office and Duty of a Minister of the Gospel*, states on the title page that it was 'first preached, and now published, with design to obviate some objections made to the author, for using *too much diligence* in the work of the ministry'. In speaking of the 'indispensable obligations' clergymen are under to a 'diligent discharge' of their duty, he says,

This is more necessary, because through our own negligence, indolence, or bad examples, the priest's office is sunk into general contempt. Ministers themselves are looked upon as covetous, crafty, designing men; as men who say and do not; and who lay burdens upon other men's shoulders, which they themselves will not touch with one of their fingers …

The more holy any man is, the more he is devoted to the service of God, the more will his conduct and principles condemn the customs and maxims of the world … [and] the more will he be despised by the men of the world …

Every clergyman is bound by all possible ties to be warm, zealous and active in preaching the everlasting gospel …

We have no other design in preaching, we have no other design in living, but to save our own soul, and the souls of them that hear us.[14]

There is no record how long this suspension lasted, but in the interval he was not idle. He travelled to Wales to preach the gospel and many who received their first religious impressions under his preaching afterwards became members of the Methodist societies. He 'preached wonderfully' at Wesley's chapel in Osmotherly and also visited nearby towns and villages. If churches were closed against him, he preached in cottages and in the open air, a practice he continued even after the storm of persecution subsided. Many were converted and he considered these itinerant labours as the happiest and most successful days of his life. Charles Roe gladly opened his drawing room for Sunday services and, in effect, he became the private chaplain of the family and any neighbours who attended. Only

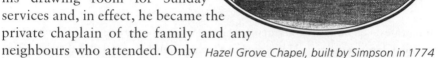

Hazel Grove Chapel, built by Simpson in 1774

later in life when his infirmities increased, particularly a 'violent pain in the head', and, as he observes, the 'Wesleyan preachers are received in all those villages [he had visited] and have formed societies', did he conclude that his exertions were no longer necessary, although he did preach elsewhere on occasion.

For a time Simpson had a small chapel at Bullock Smithy (now called Hazel Grove), which he built in 1774 at his own expense. After he moved to Christ Church, he experienced difficulty in disposing of the chapel. In 1786 he sold it to the Wesleyans and it was opened by Wesley on his eighty-third birthday, 5 April 1786.

Lady Huntingdon, seizing the opportunity, again pressed on him the offer of becoming minister of her chapel at Tunbridge Wells, but he refused a second time. She also made another offer, which Lawrence Coughlan mentions in a letter of 30 August 1774. 'A few days ago the Countess of Huntingdon sent for me … I told her how the case stood at Macclesfield: her ladyship made the answer and said if Mr Roe would build a church, she would patronise it … I have mentioned Mr Roe's intentions to several friends in London, who all said with one voice that Mr Roe may, upon the Toleration Act, build and use the Church of England service with all safety.'[15]

Charles Roe had originally offered part of his farmland, 'The Marled Bank', to the corporation for a much needed burial ground. When Simpson was suspended Roe decided to fulfil an early promise that if he should succeed in business, he would build a church as a token of his gratitude to

God; so instead of erecting a small mortuary chapel on the new burial ground, he built a 1300-seater church on his own ground, which after its consecration in 1779 was called Christ Church. However, if Roe applied for a licence to open the church under the Toleration Act, Simpson, as minister, would thereby become a dissenter, a course which many were against.

Rowland Hill, who had just had breakfast with Mr and Mrs Roe, and no doubt hearing from them the latest news, wrote to Simpson with the following advice:

Our greatest honour is to be sufferers for God. No cross no crown. Twice they have cast you out. I dare not direct … I bless the Lord I am entirely his, and daily find the portion of the outcast is a happy one indeed. However, is not your way plain? Another door opens, in which no one can molest you. Be sure of this: not a hair of your head can ever be touched for preaching under toleration: nor can it hinder you of any preferment that should offer. The canon law is nothing, having never had any parliamentary ratification … Though I preach in licensed places continually, yet more churches are open to me than I can serve. Thousands in this city flock to hear, yet multitudes go away for want of room. Ecclesiastics roar, as Luther says, like bears struck on the snout; yet this, they know, is all they can do. Your share of humility and diffidence I long for exceedingly; yet a little courage to face the devil may not be amiss. The Lord knows how difficult it is to keep measures with the wretched, much-to-be-pitied, church governors of the present day.[16]

To have taken advantage of the Toleration Act, as Rowland Hill suggested, would have turned the new church into a dissenting chapel, and to have accepted Lady Huntingdon's offer of 'protection' would have been illegal.

During these troubles and uncertainties he received several letters of advice and encouragement from his supporters, including leading men of the revival. A London layman wrote, 'I am really grieved for the poor people of Macclesfield, that they should have such an enmity to the gospel of Christ as both to shut it out of their house and no doubt out of their heart.'[17] Henry Venn, who once said to Simpson, 'I shall never forget you till I forget my Lord', wrote assuring him that he was included in an agreement between 'awakened ministers' in the Establishment 'to remember each other in their solemn preparation for each Lord's Day, by retiring on the Saturday evening, from six to seven, for prayer; to implore of the Lord, for themselves and the people, all spiritual blessings'.[18] On 4 August 1774 John Fletcher wrote from Madeley in answer to enquiries Simpson had made about his predicament.

I have sometimes preached in licensed places, but have never been censured for it. Perhaps it is because my superiors in the Church think me not worth their notice, and despair of shackling me with their *unevangelical* regularity. If the bishop were to take me to task about this piece of irregularity, I would observe—1. That the Canons of men cannot overthrow the Canons of God … 2. Before the bishop shackled me with Canons, he charged me to *seek for Christ's sheep that are dispersed abroad, and for his children, who are in the midst of this wicked world*; and these sheep, etc., I will try to gather wherever I meet with them.

Some of my parishioners went and complained to the bishop about my conventicles. I wrote to the Registrar, that I hoped his lordship who had given me the above mentioned charge at ordination, would not be against my following it; that I thought it hard the tipplers should have 20 or 30 tippling houses, the Dissenters 3 or 4 and the Papists one meeting house in my parish, undisturbed; and that I should be disturbed, because I would not have God's word confined to one house. And that, with respect to the Canons, it would be absurd to put them in force against preaching clergymen when they were set aside with respect to non-catechising, tippling, gaming, carding clergymen. That I did not desire his lordship to patronise me, in a special manner, in the use of my Christian liberty; but that I hoped he would *connive* at it …

The questions of your letter … may be properly answered by a worthy servant of Christ, the Rev. Mr. John Ryland, minister of the new chapel at Birmingham, whose case is somewhat similar to yours. This chapel was built upon the estate of a serious lady, who got it consecrated, and presented him. I design to send him your letter, and desire him to give you and your worthy patron … all the intelligence he can; only be modestly and steadily bold for God, and your enemies will be more afraid of you, than you of them; or, if God will honour you with the badge of persecution, he will comfort and bless you the more for it.[19]

In his letter, Ryland asked, 'Is it practicable to build a church or chapel in

Macclesfield for service after the Church of England form, without the consent of the vicar, and the licence of the bishop; and to secure both these, an Act of Parliament? It is not practicable.' He then made the point: 'If you erect a building without the vicar's nomination, and without the bishop's licence, you have no way but to licence it under the Toleration Act; so that you make yourself at once a Dissenter.'[20]

A month after Fletcher's letter, on 5 September 1774, the celebrated William Romaine wrote to him in a cautious tone about the way ahead. Simpson wanted the opinion of Romaine, who thought it best not to reply immediately, 'because I would have you to wait a little'.

John Fletcher of Madeley, with whom Simpson corresponded

You know I have been accustomed to such treatment as you have met with, and I have lived to see the goodness of God's dealings with me. It seems to me worth your while to wait a little upon the Lord. Don't hurry; you may take a hasty step, and repent it all your days. Wait, I say, upon the Lord; he may teach you why he silenced you. You may see it was for your good. He wanted to teach you submission, to break your own spirit, and curb your self-will; perhaps he intended to humble you, and so to fit you for more usefulness; that having done his work at Macclesfield, you might rely more upon his grace in labouring for him elsewhere …

If you follow Providence, it speaks plain. You are not shut out of the Lord's vineyard, but only called to labour in another part of it, where the door is open for you. Providences, in such cases, speak as plain as

William Romaine, who wrote to Simpson offering advice

Scripture. Pray to the Lord to make his will yours, and I doubt not in the least, but you will see your way here as plain as I do; and if you accept it, may our Divine Head bless you abundantly, and give you a large Yorkshire harvest.[21]

The reference to a 'Yorkshire harvest' refers to the perpetual curacy of Cleckheaton, which had been offered to Simpson through James Stillingfleet. At the time Romaine was staying with Richardson, the patron.

John Berridge, on 8 August 1775, when the new church in Macclesfield was under construction, also wrote to Simpson. Drawing on his own experience of when he started to itinerate, he says in his inimitable style,

As you are now doing, so did I, send letters to my friends, begging advice, but received unsatisfactory or discouraging answers. Then I saw, if I meant to itinerate, I must not confer with flesh and blood, but cast myself wholly upon the Lord …

If you are invited to go out, and feel yourself inclined to do so, take a lover's leap, neck or nothing, and commit yourself to Jesus. Ask no man's leave to preach Christ; that is unevangelical and

John Berridge of Everton, another correspondent of Simpson's

shameful. Seek not much advice about it; that is dangerous … If you are determined to be evangelically regular, i.e., secularly irregular, then expect, wherever you go, a storm will follow you, which may fright you, but will bring no real harm. Make the Lord your *whole* trust, and all will be well. Remember this, brother David! for if your heart is resting upon some human arm for support, or if your eye is squinting at it for protection, Jesus Christ will let you fall, and roll you soundly in a kennel, to teach you better manners. If you become a recruiting sergeant, you must go out—*duce et auspice Christo*. The Lord direct, assist and prosper you.[22]

While Simpson respected the often conflicting advice of his friends, he was his own man and made his own decisions. That is why, after careful consideration, he accepted Roe's offer to build him a church, not wishing, as he expressed it, to preach to a people who hated him.

Just before Roe started to build he composed a prayer, part of which reads,

In a particular manner I beg, O Lord, that thou wouldest bless and prosper all the *lawful* and laudable undertakings of thy servant, who at this time hath undertaken to build thee a house. O God, let no designs against it or him prevail, but prosper the work for the proposed end it is for, which I trust, is for the glory of thy name, and the salvation of men's souls; and I crave, O Lord, that life and health may be continued to the founder thereof, that he may live to see the desired work carried on, then finished. Likewise, O Father of mercies, I request thy majesty to spare to us the life and health of our proposed minister; furnish him with all gifts and graces of thy Holy Spirit, that he may be instrumental in thy hands for enlightening those who are in darkness, strengthening the weak, comforting all those who are in the way of Zion.[23]

He goes on to pray for all who would take part in the services and for the congregations that would assemble in the church. 'Raise up,' he says, 'from generation to generation such ministers as shall preach the truth boldly, rebuke vice freely, and speak of the faith once delivered to the saints.'

Christch Church, Macclesfield, which was built for Simpson in 1775. This is the Pownall engraving of Christ Church dated 30 April 1783. Note the elongated 'flaming urns' around the parapet and Charles Roe's obelisk/monument on the extreme left

Roe, not a man to procrastinate, set about the work in earnest, which was completed in 'so short a space of time as seven months'; that is, between May and December 1775. The tower, with its clock and ten bells, was not finished until 1777. The new church was 'an elegant and beautiful structure', with two side galleries and a gallery at the west end, and 'sufficiently

capacious to contain two thousand persons'[24] (actually 1300 was the seating capacity). It had a magnificent organ, which came from a London theatre and on which Handel had often played. The organist, Aeneas Maclardie, was an eccentric but talented musician. John Wesley, on visiting Macclesfield in 1786, found a people 'much alive to God' and referred to the organ as 'one of the finest-toned I ever heard; and the congregation singing

A balsa-wood model of the original 3-decker pulpit in Christ Church. It was made by students of the Manchester School of Architecture

with it make a sweet harmony'.[25] The pulpit was over 3½ metres high, allowing the preacher a commanding view of his congregation.

As promised the new church was built at Roe's sole expense (it cost about £6000), although others wanted to contribute. A rich lady in the neighbourhood, also a supporter of Simpson, pleaded with Roe to accept her donation towards the building, but he refused it. She then offered to purchase the bells for the church, but again Roe declined her gift, erecting the bells, along with everything else, at his own cost. A rumour soon spread that Roe was not as generous as it might appear, for he was really building the church for his son, who had just entered Oxford University, and Simpson was just a stand-in. This falsehood was quashed on the completion of the church, when he gave Simpson a deed for life. A parsonage was also built for Simpson on Park Green on freehold land donated by John Ryle, the Methodist mill owner and banker, so the 'bishops had no access to lord it over him'.

The church was opened on Christmas Day 1775. In the course of the sermon to mark the occasion Simpson, only too aware of the controversy surrounding the new church, said to the congregation,

Away then, my brethren, with all party names and uncharitable distinctions. Let the only name of which you are ambitious, be, that of *Christian*, and the only religion after which you aspire, be that of the Bible. Let others talk about sects and parties. Let others dispute about principles and doctrines; but let it be our daily aim, study and endeavour, to grow more and more in humility, in meekness, in knowledge, in love, in gentleness, in goodness and benevolence ...

It is with a design to promote this true catholic, evangelical and saving religion;—it is with a design to advance the real interest and happiness of the people of this town and neighbourhood that this building, at a large expense, has been erected. It is not to promote the low selfish interests of a sect or party, but the general happiness, the general salvation of our fellow creatures around ...

The intention ... of erecting this building was to advance the glory of God, the furtherance of the gospel, the reformation of the disobedient, and the salvation of souls ...

Now, if but one person should be thus brought to God—if but one soul should be converted and saved, in consequence of this church being erected, the money, the time, the pains, is well spent: for one soul is of more real value than all the world. But, my brethren, we hope for greater things. We hope the Lord will favour us with his power and assistance; and not only one, but many—many—many—will be turned from darkness to light, and from the power of Satan unto God. I cannot be easy or satisfied, while one disobedient, unconverted person remains among you.[26]

In the same sermon he paid a glowing tribute to his dear friend Charles Roe, and acknowledged elsewhere that the 'principal part of the genteel fortune which his family and children at present enjoy was poured into his lap after he began to build this church for God. This he himself saw, acknowledged, and frequently spoke of with tears of gratitude ... I have rarely known such a flight of public spirit, on the one hand, and of God's remunerating goodness, on the other, in any age or nation.'[27] In the sermon, he said,

Has he [Roe] not been, upon all occasions, the town's benefactor? Has he not been instrumental in the hands of God of enlarging your borders? ... Has he not fed, for many years, hundreds of your poor with bread? Have not arts and manufactures arisen and improved by his means, and under his fostering hand? Do not thousands of pounds every year circulate through your hands, or at least through the hands of the gentlemen of the town, all owing to his industry, ingenuity and influence? And is there no gratitude, no kind returns due for favours so many and benefits so extensive? ...

He saw your souls in danger. He lamented the ignorance, wickedness and profaneness, which reigned amongst many ... He pitied your condition and contrived a way of relieving you. I have heard him bewail your ignorance and danger, and express the ardent desire he had of serving you in your spiritual interests. This he has done. He has built you a house. Yea, though he has so large a family [a wife and eleven children], his public spirit has built you a house of God, at several thousand pounds expense, and that too in less time than was almost ever known. Was it done to serve me, after I was excluded from the other Church? No: I had opportunities of going elsewhere. Was it done to answer his own private interest? No: He always expected to be a considerable loser by the undertaking. Was it done out of resentment, and to satisfy a party spirit? No: This could not be, because he had intended to build several years before party arose .... His motive ... was ... to advance the glory of God, the furtherance of the gospel, the reformation of his fellow creatures, and the salvation of souls.[28]

One of the opportunities that Simpson had of 'going elsewhere' came from John Thornton, who offered to procure him better preferment, a preferment that Simpson refused because 'divine providence seemed to have placed me where I was, and I could not think of quitting my station merely for the sake of a better living; till the time came that the same providence should call me away'.[29]

Three months after the opening of Christ Church, Simpson preached a sermon from Romans 14:17 that caused Hester Ann Roe to exclaim, 'O the blessedness of this inward kingdom! With streaming eyes, and a heart overflowing with love, I could claim this portion mine; mine in possession, and mine for ever!'[30] During the course of the year she visited Simpson and enjoyed open and encouraging fellowship with him, which she recorded in her diary.

I called at Mr Simpson's and found him alone this evening. He asked me many questions respecting my experience; and I freely told him what the Lord had done, and is doing for me. He said, 'I wish I felt the same. I long for it, and believe it is the privilege of the children of God, though too few enjoy it: but the promises of God imply, and his precepts require it. Let no one discourage you, Miss Roe; for what you experience is of God. You need never lose it; and I hope you will pray that I may attain it.' My soul truly rejoiced to hear him speak thus. Lord, baptize thy servant with thy Holy Spirit, and let him be made pure in heart—the temple of indwelling God.[31]

Bishop Markham, because the church was not put under episcopal jurisdiction and because of Simpson's Methodism, refused to consecrate it; instead, he simply ignored it and acted as though it did not exist. However, in 1778, with the death of Thomas Hewson, the prime curacy of the old church (St Michael's) became vacant, the nomination of which was appended to the office of mayor *pro tempore*. Matters were brought to a crisis, when Rowland Gould, the mayor, and Simpson's friend, the chief magistrate, offered it to Simpson, who gladly accepted. Many parishioners were unhappy. 'Every stratagem within the reach of human ingenuity was tried, and every effort that inveterate malice could prompt was made to prevent his induction. His adversaries rallied *all* their strength.'[32] At last they sent a petition, with seventeen accusations attached to it, to the new bishop of Chester, Beilby Porteus, the first bishop to show any favour towards evangelicals. Upon examination Porteus could only discover *one charge*, that he was a Methodist and that his preaching promoted the spread of Methodism. In a letter to his lordship, Simpson, with his usual intrepidity, alluded to the alleged offence.

This is true. My method is to preach the great truths and doctrines and precepts of the gospel in as plain and earnest and affectionate a manner as I am able. Persons of different ranks, persuasions and characters come to hear. Some hereby have been convinced of the error of their ways, see their guilt and the danger they are in, and become seriously concerned about their salvation. The change is soon discovered, they meet with one or another who invite them to attend the preachings and meetings among the Methodists, and hence their number is increased to a considerable degree. This is the truth. I own the fact. I have often thought of it; but I confess myself unequal to the difficulty. What would your lordship advise? [It appears the bishop advised him to decline the offer.][33]

His enemies were furious that the bishop had not immediately refused him, but Simpson remained calm and dignified throughout. A proposal was made to his opponents, stating that he would relinquish the prime curacy of the old church, to which he had been presented, provided he could secure the consecration of the new church and be regularly inducted as incumbent. To this his enemies agreed.

Christ Church was finally consecrated in 1779 and on 31 December Simpson was licensed to it by Bishop Porteus. He resigned his curacy and for the rest of his life was allowed to continue his ministrations without interruption or hindrance. 'Thus ended,' says Gaulter, 'a succession of opposition, almost unexampled in modern history.'[34] Interestingly, within a few years, because of his benevolence and consistent piety, several of his most zealous adversaries had become his keenest supporters, receiving great benefit from his preaching.

Beilby Porteus, bishop of Chester, and the first bishop to show any favour towards Evangelicals

The conflict he endured appears to have made such an impression on his mind that before his death he determined to leave the Established Church. He recognised the 'spirit of error, impiety and persecution' in the Church of England's clergy, 'preying upon her vitals and hastening her dissolution'; and was convinced, that 'those among her advocates were her worst adversaries, who were most voluble in boasting of her excellencies, while wilfully blind to all her defects and blemishes; and who, while lamenting the increase of dissenters, and Methodists, would banish and stigmatise the only men qualified to defend her outworks and promote her internal welfare.'[35] In his own words, he lamented that the Establishment had for so long boasted 'of the excellence of our church' and made so many compliments about the 'unparalleled purity of our hierarchy',

that a stranger would be led to conclude, to be sure we must be the holiest, happiest, and most flourishing church upon the face of the earth. Whereas, when you go into our most stately and magnificent cathedrals, and other sacred edifices, you find them almost empty and forsaken. At best all is deadness and lukewarmness both with priest and people. In various instances, there is little more appearance of devotion than in a Jew's synagogue. Go where you will through the kingdom, one or the other of these is very generally the case, except where the officiating clergyman is strictly moral in his conduct, serious, earnest and lively in his manner, and evangelical in his doctrine. Where this, however, happens to be so, the stigma of Methodism is almost universally affixed to his character, and his name is had for a proverb of reproach, in proportion to his zeal and usefulness, by the sceptics and infidels all around, in which they are frequently joined to the rich, the fashionable, and the gay, with the bishop and the clergy at their head.[36]

Once the furore had died down and he was allowed to work in peace, his ministry was attended 'with one continued flow of success'. A large congregation gathered to sit under his preaching, many were brought to a saving knowledge of Christ, and Christians were united and grounded in the faith. This is not to say that there were no more trials for him to face, but as he looked forward it was not so much the storm, but the calm after the storm that he saw. The night of trial was ready to yield to a day of blessing.

(3) Macclesfield: Years of Triumph

The last twenty years of Simpson's ministry 'was the brightest period of his life … Every day he became more zealous and laborious, and was honoured with a proportionate increase of usefulness.'[1] All denominations of Christians respected him, and even those who could not agree with his creed were forced to venerate his character. So general was the esteem in which he was held, that during his last sickness prayers were offered on his behalf, not only in his own church, but among the dissenters and Methodists, and even in St Michael's.

At the start of his gospel work he was paid only £60 a year, but during that time, according to his own admission, he 'never took more pains in the ministry'. After he married and had children his income from the Church 'never amounted to £120' and yet he was happy. 'I have laboured hard, studied hard, and, probably, have been as useful and well satisfied with my condition as the fattest rector in all the diocese of Chester.' Even if he had been offered a living of £500 or £1000, he doubted whether he would have been more content or a more useful minister of the gospel. 'It is much more likely,' he said, 'I should have been seriously injured, should have composed myself to rest, and cried with the rich fool, "Soul, thou hast much goods laid up for many years; take thine ease, eat, drink, and be merry."'[2] In his poverty, he made the prayer of John Jortin his own, 'I have been poor, according to thy good pleasure, but contented. I have had no dignities: thou hast withheld them, and I have not thought them even worthy of a wish.'[3]

In order to encourage his congregation to worship he compiled *A Collection of Psalms and Hymns and Spiritual Songs, for the Use of Christians of Every Denomination,* a large work of more than 600 hymns, psalms and anthems, which curiously includes quotations from Shakespeare, Spenser and other poets, all emphasising the worth of music in worship. It was first published in 1776, but a new shorter edition appeared in 1795 under the title *Select Psalms and Hymns.* In the first edition he introduced some 'divine poems' 'for the improvement and entertainment of young people, and those among the poor whose minds have happily taken a religious turn, but who are not able to purchase many books'.[4] In subsequent editions these 'extras' were omitted.

Simpson enjoyed well-written hymns with a good chorus and grand resonant phrasing. In an appealing preface, which highlights the author's love of music, anthems and organs, he says, 'Brisk, solemn, lively tunes are best adapted to awaken holy affections. Avoid therefore such as are light, frothy and fantastic, and let all the congregation join together in one grand chorus. Such words, such tunes, such singing as leaves us dull, stupid and languid, answers no valuable end whatever. They are neither pleasing to God, nor profitable to man.' He admits that the organ, if played badly, 'is rather hurtful to devotion than otherwise', but 'in good hands and under judicious management' it can produce 'most rare and beautiful effects upon the mind'. He disagrees with those 'gloomy beings' (men such as Romaine), 'who explode all music, vocal and instrumental', and wonders 'what such persons mean to make of themselves when they arrive at heaven where there is an eternal "Hallelujah", sung in full chorus before the throne of God'.[5]

On 14 September 1777 an earthquake hit Macclesfield at about eleven o'clock, during the Sunday morning service. It was described at the time as a 'smart shock', which extended through a circuit of more than 300 miles. According to Hester Roe, Christ Church

... rocked like a cradle; and nearly threw some people, when kneeling, on their faces; and the noise, for a few moments, was like thunder. Some believed the Church was fallen at the steeple end, and therefore flew in crowds to the opposite doors, shrieking and crying for mercy. Some fainted, and were trampled nearly to death; others were bruised much; and some did not recover the fright. I was enabled to exhort those around me to be still, and look unto the God of grace for salvation, which they had too long neglected. Many were deeply awakened by this awful providence, and never found rest afterwards, till they found it in the manifested love of a blessed Redeemer.[6]

The steeple, 'an uncommonly high tower', had recently been finished and the whole congregation, fearing it was about to fall on them, fled in confusion. The passage of the church was immediately blocked and the groans from the frightened and trapped were described as dreadful. Simpson stood alone at the communion table in the chancel, trying to calm the panic by urging his congregation to retake their seats. Many were injured, suffering broken bones and concussion, but thankfully no lives were lost. Quite a few were so alarmed by the terrifying circumstances and so impressed by their deliverance from danger that they became seriously concerned about the salvation of their souls. That afternoon Simpson preached a moving sermon on the 'divine visitation'.

One of the first enterprises that Simpson set up was the establishment of charity schools (1778). At first he encouraged some of his supporters among the educated classes to gather the poorer children into their own homes and teach them free of charge. As the numbers increased a silk throwster's shed was hired and an evening school started, so children employed in the silk and cotton factories could attend after work. Soon several evening schools were opened in the town. Some of the teachers were paid 2/6 a week, which was donated by wealthy patrons. On Sunday the children were accompanied to church by their teachers. For several years Simpson managed the schools on his own, but when it was suggested that the schools could be made more general, he willingly agreed to give them up to a committee of gentlemen from the town, only stipulating that the children were to be taken to church every Sunday and instructed in writing. In all from four to five hundred children were taught in this way.

In 1794 Simpson felt the management of the schools was not as efficient as it might be, so he called in inspectors to visit them every Lord's Day and to make a report once a month. This prepared the way for a Sunday School, which was opened on 1 May 1796 by John Whitaker, a twenty-four year old Methodist, who had been previously taken on as a teacher in Simpson's charity schools and paid a small retainer for his services. The Sunday School was carried on solely by volunteers. It continued long after Simpson's death and afforded upwards of 2000 children free education. Some of the children, after they had grown up, became Sunday School teachers themselves. John Corry wrote that

… the personal exertions of Mr Simpson, most essentially contributed to the success of [the Sunday School]. His ready, powerful, and commanding eloquence, was poured forth like a flowing stream, in behalf of the juvenile and susceptible mind; and the rich and the poor were unanimous in their approbation of so cheap and effectual a method of imparting useful knowledge not only without impediment to the pursuits of the industrious, but actually affording a most pleasing and profitable recreation to the teachers and their pupils.[7]

However, Simpson was not the founder of Sunday Schools, as some have claimed, for he himself said, 'Mr [Robert] Raikes of Gloucester was the happy man who first started the idea of Sunday Schools, and if any person was to receive honour according to the good he is of to society, no man in England is so justly entitled to have a statue of marble or of gold erected to his memory as he is.'[8]

About 1781 Simpson opened a co-educational school for young people initially in his own home on Park Green, which helped

Robert Raikes, the founder of Sunday Schools

The memorial tablet to Charles Roe in Christ Church. It is the work of the sculptor John Bacon the Elder and was finished in 1784. It is made of marble and consists of the figure of the genius of the useful arts, who holds a medallion of Roe in one hand and the model of a wheel in the other. The three compartments below show the first silk mill erected in Macclesfield, the north-east view of Christ Church, and the copper works at Liverpool.

supplement his income. Most of the work he took on himself. At one period the school was so successful that there were more than 160 scholars attending it, and in the winter months they would study for an hour or two by candlelight before breakfast. In later years, when talking about this time of his life, he thought the early discipline of the school had been too severe, but Edward Parsons points out that Simpson's 'method of illustration in the readings, which formed part of his school exercises, was always so engaging, that they generally sat down to that exercise as the most agreeable relaxation'.[9]

The monument to Charles Roe in the churchyard before it was dismantled in 1962

One of those educated by Simpson was Edward Oakes, who was converted at fourteen after hearing a sermon by the Wesleyan minister Joseph Benson. He became a local preacher at eighteen and later joined the Wesleyan itinerancy, exercising an active circuit ministry in England before severe asthma forced him into superannuation in 1834.

In the same year as Simpson opened the school, and five and a half years after his settlement in the new church, he suffered a double loss in the death of his father at Hutton Rudby and his friend and patron Charles Roe, who died after a short illness on 3 May 1781 at the age of 67. Hester Ann says, 'I went to my uncle's this morning, May 3. He lay all night quite composed, and I have great hope he is escaped to endless life.'[10] After his death Roe was 'carried in great pomp by his own carriage and horses' to the new church, where Simpson interred him in a vault he had only recently prepared for himself. A marble monument, sculptured by John Bacon the Elder, was erected by his widow and children. Part of the inscription reads:

It pleased the ALMIGHTY to bless his various labours and benevolent designs. His grateful heart delighted to acknowledge the mercies he received. GOD was in all his thoughts. And actuated by the purest sentiments of genuine devotion, which burnt steadily through his life, and the brighter as he approached the FOUNTAIN OF LIGHT, he dedicated to the service of his MAKER, a part of that increase his bounty had bestowed; erecting and endowing at his sole expense, the elegant structure which encloses this monument.[11]

These sad losses were partly compensated for by the birth of his son David on 10 April.

In 1782, for the benefit of women, he instituted a female friendly society, unprecedented at the time. It was always a favourite object of his care, and when he first established it he engaged some respectable ladies to qualify themselves as honorary members. Every week he held an evening lecture, where he first gave out a hymn, then prayed, and concluded with admonitions for the improvement of their morals. His advice was, 'Be careful … the character of a woman is like glass; if once injured it can never be restored.' It was succeeded by two other similar institutions, which he watched over with great zeal, and every year, in their anniversary sermon, he urged the members to a diligent regard of those duties which 'adorn and elevate the female character, both in the higher and humbler walks of life'.[12]

Once the new Sunday School was established he visited it once a week, along with his curate, to catechise and instruct the senior scholars. Before long many strangers wanted to attend. Because of the growing numbers, he started on Wednesday evenings a course of lectures on John Bunyan's *Pilgrim's Progress*, particularly to win the interest of the young people in the town. The service was conducted in an upper room of a large factory. The first meeting, held on 14 February 1798, was so crowded at the end nearest the door that one of the middle supporting beams gave way and many were thrown through the floor with such violence that the floor beneath was broken and the

John Bunyan

sufferers were hurled to the ground. The cries and groans heard in the darkness were horrific. One young woman survived only a few hours and many others (about 70) were terribly mangled. The injured were well looked after and a generous subscription was made, which provided them with much needed medical support to aid their recovery. Thankfully, Simpson and others escaped unhurt because they were standing at either end of the room, where the walls remained firm.

Simpson was deeply grieved by the accident, but satisfied that the lectures fulfilled an important role for good decided not to stop them. He continued them on the ground floor, a safer but less commodious part of the building. A serious and thoughtful crowd assembled regularly for about nine months until he was forced to give up a few months before his death because of a severe 'paralytic attack'. He noticed, with delight, that his greatest success was with the young, who not only revered him as their pastor, but enjoyed his cheerfulness and kindness to them, and confided in him as their friend.

Another terrible incident occurred the same year. On 2 June a large congregation, including Simpson, assembled at Wesley's Chapel in Sunderland Street to hear Dr Coke preach.

As he was about to announce his text, a sudden panic seized some of the persons present. Their apprehension that the roof was about to fall in was quickly communicated to others, and soon the whole congregation was a prey to it. In the confusion that ensued, some rushed wildly out at the doors, others flung themselves from the windows, and many were trampled under foot. A person who was seen to leap from one of the gallery windows, fell upon a poor woman below, and so caused her instant death. Six lives were lost altogether, and many persons were seriously hurt.[13]

Simpson did his best to allay the panic of those near him, but to no avail. The following Sunday, in order to deepen the impressions the catastrophe had produced, he preached a sermon with the title 'God's Choice the Best for his People'.

Even after he was settled in his own church, Simpson did not feel inhibited to preach the gospel in other places. He preached 'special sermons' at Sheffield and other industrial centres, and for several years, on

Hazdgrove

the invitation of Cornelius Bayley, he preached at St James's Church in Manchester during race week to large and attentive congregations. Every three months he went to Bullock Smithy near Stockport and 'scarcely ever without some visible success'. On one of these occasions he preached from Daniel 5:27: 'Thou art weighed in the balances and found wanting.'

After making a solemn pause, every eye being fixed upon him in breathless expectation, he demanded, with a dignity peculiar to himself, that his hearers should permit conscience, for once, to bear its faithful testimony as to their individual condition before God. He inquired whether, if at that moment, they were to be weighed in the balances of Divine Justice, they would not, assuredly, be found wanting? 'Conviction,' it is said, 'flashed upon the people like lightning; and every part of the assembly was vocal with cries and groans.'[14]

It was at Bullock Smithy in 1786 that Simpson, the founder, assisted John Wesley at the opening of a chapel. He read the church service and Wesley preached from Acts 2:4. After the service forty of them adjourned to an inn where they dined. According to Luke Tyerman, Simpson 'became one of Wesley's sincerest and warmest friends',[15] and they agreed on many of the fundamental issues of religion. Wesley would have loved Simpson to become one of his travelling preachers and he regarded his ministry 'as a model for his ideas to reform the Church of England, it being evangelical and urban rather than staid and largely rural'.[16]

Wesley preached at Macclesfield approximately twenty-eight times and Christ Church was the only Anglican Church in the county to invite him openly. He preached at Christ Church in April 1777, when he described the new church as 'far the most elegant that I have seen in the kingdom'. Simpson read prayers and Wesley preached on Hebrews 11, and 'many felt their want of the faith there spoken of'.[17] Five years later, on Good Friday 29 March 1782, both men distributed the sacrament to 'about thirteen hundred persons. While we were administering,' wrote Wesley, 'I heard a low, soft, solemn sound, just like that of an Aeolian harp. It continued five or six minutes, and so affected many, that they could not refrain from tears. It then gradually died away.'[18] In 1784 Simpson attended Wesley's conference, and in April 1788 the two men were together in Oldham Street

Methodist Chapel, Manchester, ministering to 'about a thousand communicants; and surely God was among them'.[19] Simpson's respect for Wesley's judgement probably suspended for years his rising inclination to withdraw from the Church of England.

On occasions Simpson travelled to London, where he stayed with his friend De Coetlogon or at some clerical club. On one of these visits he listened to Augustus Toplady preach at the Lock Chapel, and later in life gave his opinion on what he had heard.

He treated all those who could not swallow his principles as mire in the street ... [I] thought him very harsh and inconclusive in his reasonings. I said

Augustus Toplady, a forthright Calvinist

to myself, whether the doctrine of election is true, or not, this is not the way to defend it. Some of my readers will probably be of opinion, that it would have been much to this gentleman's honour to have retracted several of his doctrines, and unsaid many of the intemperate things which he advanced in the course of his polemical career.[20]

Simpson never wasted a moment and was always looking for some way to benefit his parishioners. By early rising and hard work, he managed to publish many volumes—thirteen in all—some of them large ones, which not only speak of the extensive nature and variety of his research, but also the character of his heart. His largest work is *Sacred Literature* (1788–91) in four volumes, in which he shows the 'Scriptures to be superior to the most celebrated writings of antiquity'. He gives 500 testimonies from persons of all ages and ranks in society to support his case, and creates a moral and theological repository of great use to ordinary Christians. This particular work endorses his own opinion that he was a compiler rather than an original thinker, who had a gift for arranging relevant material.

Finding the theatre to be pernicious in its influence and on the occasion of a visit from a company of comedians to the town, he wrote a pamphlet on the uses and abuses of *Stage Entertainments* (1788), 'inscribed to the mayor and justice of the peace of the borough of Macclesfield', which was so successful that it 'almost overturned theatrical representations in Macclesfield for that winter'. He also wrote against Joseph Priestley's *Essay on Fatalism*, which had been attacked by Joseph Benson, an itinerant preacher and one time headmaster of Tiverton College in Wales. Priestley, when asked why he did not answer Benson's book, replied that he would not contend with a layman. Simpson heard about Priestley's excuse and challenged him to 'write with a clergyman'.

Joseph Priestley, whose 'Essay on Fatalism' Simpson strongly opposed

Simpson's most popular work in which he attacked the Protestant hierarchy with 'satirical acrimony' was *A Plea for Religion and the Sacred Writings*, which was 'addressed to the disciples of Thomas Paine and wavering Christians of every persuasion'. It was first issued in 1797. Two editions were printed in his lifetime, and many more have been printed in London and America since his death. John Williams remarks that *A Plea for Religion* has been 'in the highest and best sense remarkably useful. Through its instrumentality many an infidel has been reclaimed; many a believer established; and many a sinner, not merely convinced of the error of his ways, but led effectively to the Saviour.'[21] This was certainly true of a court physician, who came to a knowledge of the truth through reading Simpson's *Plea*. After his death a member of a literary society was saved from adopting the views of Socinianism through a careful study of Simpson's arguments, along with several others, including a Socinian minister who gave up his charge as a result.

Simpson's writings are similar in character, and he used wisely his large library, which contained many useful books of ancient and modern literature. He always endeavoured to promote the study of the Scriptures, which 'alone is perfect truth'. His advice was:

Read your Bibles, and read them daily till you love to read. Pray daily over them, and pray till you love to pray ... Read them in the original language if you can: if not, in our own excellent translation. Read them with fervent and persevering prayer. Read them frequently upon your knees; and as much as possible, divert yourself of all prejudice of mind and every preconceived opinion. I would recommend them, moreover, to be read without notes or illustrations of any kind, or at least let them be very concise and free from party rage. Comments and illustrations usually do more harm than good, by drawing our attention too much from the text itself ... We are all too prone to bring our own principles to the Bible, rather than come to it with the simplicity of little children to learn from it.[22]

Study and meditate upon the Word of God. Its promises are large and full; its threats infinitely awful; and its precepts divinely pure. Study to conform your whole life to its directions. Jesus Christ you will find to be the sum and substance of it ...

Young and old get Bibles. Read them with humble, earnest prayer to God for the enlightening influences of his Holy Spirit to enable you to understand them. Read to practise; read to obey. Read to mend the heart, not merely to fill the head.[23]

His aim was 'to vindicate [the Bible's] authority, to allure by its beauties, and to demonstrate the happiness, which is inseparable from its cordial belief ... What he wrote was profusely illustrated, either by anecdotes or narratives, or poetry, or the opinions of others. His annotations upon some subjects, furnish a bibliographer's manual.'[24]

His general reading was extensive and varied, but always directed to the understanding and defence of the truth. His choices were determined partly by duty and preference, and partly by a confusion he had long experienced on some subjects of supreme importance. In his preparation for the press, there was nothing unnatural or pretentious about him. He was only concerned about the salvation of men, and with that end in view his style of writing was both plain and pointed. He much preferred to reach the common man, than to please those with refined tastes. He said of certain religious tracts drawn up for the poor, 'They are too well written; these *finished* things are not *striking* enough; a person must be content to forfeit some of his fame as an elegant writer, if he would be useful.'[25] Occasionally, it is true to say, his style was a little *too* plain, but it was always frank and pointed. Its clarity added greatly to its force, and the reader could not but be impressed with the sincerity and grace of the author.

His love of Hebrew is seen not just in the advice he gave to Bible readers, but in his comments on female education, which are an example of his direct and plain style, unacceptable in our 'politically correct' day.

If they could be prevailed upon, after the acquirement of English, to spend the fourth part of their time in learning Hebrew, to enable them to converse with God in his own dialect, which they usually spend unnecessarily a-bed in a morning, or at the toilet, the assembly, or the card table, or in reading, or sighing over those wretched pretty things called novels, which so soften and enervate their minds, as to render them unutterably incapable of all virtuous and noble exertions, it would not fail but they would reap a rich harvest of profit and satisfaction.[26]

Many of his friends were amazed at his industry. Robinson of Leicester, himself a prolific writer, said to him,

When I look at *you* and consider the quality and variety of work you are able to attend to, I am ashamed of my own negligence and inactivity. I desire to bless and praise our gracious God, who still supports and prospers you in his service, and hath given you a pen to write, as well as a tongue to speak in defence of his truth and in attestation of his grace. I am astonished that you have leisure enough to enter so thoroughly into these subjects; and that, with all your other ministerial engagements, you should stand forth, with so much ability to repel the insolent attacks of the adversaries of our faith.[27]

His knowledge of medicine and law he used for the health and interest of his people, legally representing them when necessary and arguing on their behalf for the smallpox vaccination. In this connection he wrote an important discourse encouraging inoculation, which was written to the four surgeons in the town. In concluding the sermon, he said,

If you are satisfied, my brethren, it is your duty to give your dear offspring this chance of escaping a premature death, call in a surgeon to your assistance. If you are not able to pay a surgeon for his advice and attendance, go and tell the gentlemen of the faculty your desire and circumstances, and beg their assistance gratis … If you want further advice, come to me, and I will advise you in the best manner I am able, and make you every assistance in my power, without either fee or reward.[28]

He supported the poor and visited the sick, providing both groups with medicines; he gave a large collection of books to be freely used in the district; he entrusted quantities of religious tracts to travelling salesmen, often with little hope of receiving payment for them; and once he lent £500 to a hat manufacturer in the town. He set up scholarships to The King's School and a young man's Bible reading fellowship, and was always gentle and polite to those seeking advice on spiritual matters. Every Monday afternoon and for one hour on other days, except Saturdays and Sundays, his study door was open, and the 'diseased, the needy, the disconsolate, and the oppressed crowded in to receive relief from him; and to their great felicity, were dismissed with the oil and the wine poured into their wounds'.[29] In his *A Key to the Prophecies*, the author of the short memoir which precedes the work sums up Simpson's love for others by saying, 'Many times has he caused the fears to be dried up from the eyes of the fatherless, and the widow's heart to dance for joy.'[30] In one of the elegies written after his death, the writer draws attention to Simpson, 'the Good Samaritan'.

Before our eyes divine religion brought,
Thy life presenting what thy doctrine taught.
Vast stores of learning deep adorn'd thy mind,
And bounteous nature equal treasures join'd ...
He mourn'd with those who pain or want endure,
A guardian-angel to the sick and poor;
Where the two best of charities he join'd,
To cure the body, and to heal the mind.[31]

It was Simpson's sympathetic attention to the welfare of the industrial classes that was partly the cause of his popularity and he 'proved to be a strong anchorman in the midst of a completely new form of industrial urban community'.[32] A friend of Tim Brinton's once said, 'Week after week, when David Simpson had climbed into his high 3-decker pulpit, he had earned the right to preach to the congregation sitting below him and for them to listen to whatever he had to say to them.'³³

Throughout his ministry Simpson wholeheartedly supported the fervent and biblical preaching of the gospel and opposed any system that restricted the full proclamation of Christ, and yet no one could describe him as a bigot. On the one hand, he wanted his fellow clergy to 'out-preach, out-pray, out-live, and out-labour the clergy of all the different denominations'; on the other, it did not matter to him to which denomination preachers belonged as long as they upheld the truth. On one occasion, he confessed

… though a clergyman of the Establishment, I see no evil in joining for public worship or social intercourse, with any of the denominations of Christians. I hear what passes with candour, join where I approve, and reject whatever appears contrary to Scripture, and the plain dictates of sound reason and common sense. I am well aware this comes not up to the full standard of orthodoxy. But if such a conduct constitutes a bad Churchman, I feel not anxious to be accounted a good one.³⁴

When the Independents were trying to establish themselves in Macclesfield, rather than ignore or oppose them, as many did, he offered them the use of his school room so they could hold services without interference. Later he visited the Independent Chapel to hear Joseph Smith preach. He was on very friendly terms with the Methodist ministers of the circuit and his house was always open to members of that society. He often went, with his family, to the Methodist meetings, where he sat in a retired part of the chapel and joined in the worship, and at the end of 1797 he attended 'the renewing of the covenant' at the Methodist Chapel along with a huge congregation. One of his friends rightly said of him, 'I have never yet met with any one, in whom candour and impartiality were more conspicuous; he would readily allow to all, every thing which could possibly be advanced in favour of their tenets or mode of worship, and cheerfully gave them the right hand of fellowship.'³⁵

In stature Simpson was about average size. He was 'comely and well proportioned' and his eyes were uncommonly bright, piercing and expressive. He wore plain clothes, a wig and a clerical hat, which he cocked in a manner common among clergymen. He kept a horse, rode boldly and without fatigue, and enjoyed exercise, all of which spurred on his itinerant preaching. In character he was a Christian and a gentleman, pious and polite, with a keen sense of humour and a tenacity of purpose; in the pulpit he was natural and commanding, and was noted for holding up a large Bible when he preached. Once he threw the Bible cushion at an old lady who had fallen asleep in one of his sermons, exclaiming, 'No one sleeps whilst David Simpson preaches.' As in his writings, his remarks were designed to strike the conscience. For instance, speaking to mill hands, he said, 'Come now, try if any of you have waste silk concealed about your aprons or in your pockets, and thus have cheated your masters.'[36]

He had good enunciation and a well-disposed voice. According to competent judges, his reading was excellent. 'The modulations of his voice were so well disposed, and his emphasis so correctly laid, that illiterate people have expressed their opinion of his reading the lessons in the service, by saying, "that it was like an explanation of the chapter as he went along".'[37] One individual is said to have been converted simply by hearing him recite a verse of Isaac Watts:

Let those *refuse to sing*
That never knew our God;
But children of the heavenly King,
May speak their joys abroad.

He always read his 'beautifully written' sermons, not through choice, but because of a lack of confidence. Once he was preaching a charity sermon at Congleton extemporaneously when his thoughts became confused and his mind went blank and he had to stop abruptly. After that he preferred to write out in full what he wanted to say. However, his manner in preaching was intensely earnest and plain, with a natural use of illustration, although his zeal 'sometimes hurried him into singularities which were ludicrous'. He possessed the gift of making the Bible so simple that all could understand its message, which, along with an uncompromising faithfulness to the word, made his congregations listen to him with 'an unusually deep interest'. One of his pupils, Joseph Taylor, who later became the headmaster of Stourbridge Grammar School, said, 'His preaching was pathetic and powerful: his style clear, nervous and manly, but his method of composing his sermons for the pulpit somewhat remarkable: he always wrote his sermon before he chose the text.'[38]

The subjects on which he loved to preach were typically evangelical: 'the apostasy and depravity of man; his redemption by Christ; the indispensable necessity of regeneration; of faith in Christ; and the fruits of righteousness'.[39] In his preparations he was unashamed to 'borrow' ideas from men he respected, often noting their names on his MS. Davies was one of his favourite authors of sermons and he was thought to resemble him in many ways. He also enjoyed Ogden, Jortin, Horsley and Bellamy; and often spoke of Robert Walker and Witherspoon with great approval. He highly praised Butler's *Analogy* and said, as a recommendation, that 'amidst all the fluctuations he had experienced from the contradictory, and plausible opinions of men, no other volume gave him so much satisfaction'.[40]

In what he said, he was not interested in popular appeal, but urged all to repent. His purpose, in his own words, was to 'humble the sinner; exalt the Saviour; to promote holiness', and he was not prepared to change. 'Gentlemen, you possess authority sufficient to change me *for* another preacher, whenever you please, but you have no power to change me *into* another preacher. If you do not convince my understanding that I am in error, you can never induce me to alter my method of preaching.'[41] Once, while out riding with a friend about three months before his death, he said confidently, I have 'never withheld any truth either from fear, or with a desire to obtain the favour of any man'.[42] His uncompromising stand for the truth made it 'almost impossible for any one to be inattentive or trifling; a sacred awe generally rested upon the whole congregation. Everyone saw that he was powerfully affected with the awful warnings, and encouraging invitations, he gave to others.'[43]

Simpson's church was nearly always packed, and the Lord's table was commonly attended by six or seven hundred communicants. Many, when the weather was good, travelled from five to ten miles to hear him. One man walked forty miles to sit under his ministry. Scores of ordinary people were affected by Simpson's preaching. One of his servants was converted through his ministry, so was a Sheffield excise man; another, who lived far from Macclesfield, testified, 'I never heard anyone preach like him.' On one occasion, a young man, after listening to one of Simpson's searching sermons, returned home and actually knelt on the Bible to curse him; but when he was near death this same individual wanted both the preacher's presence and prayers. John Metcalfe, the famous blind road engineer ('Blind Jack'), was once conducted to Simpson's church, where

… either by a remarkable coincidence, or (as the narrator believed) because he noticed the blind man seated among his hearers, [the preacher] dwelt impressively upon the goodness of God in compensating persons deprived of one faculty, by increasing the strength and keenness of other powers. His words not only affected the old man, but arrested the attention of his youthful grandson, who was with him, and who related the circumstance on his death bed in the year 1865.[44]

On New Year's Eve 1798, Simpson's daughter wrote, 'We were soon waked out of our first sleep by a number of the new church congregation singing a hymn called "Hosannah". We afterwards found it was intended to express their approbation of my father's sermon in the morning.'[45]

And so Simpson prospered through the years of triumph, which were soon to be replaced with the ultimate victory. The twilight of his life was not going to be easy, but God is ever faithful. As he looked beyond the river of death, his confidence was not in the fruitfulness of his ministry or the purity of his character, but in the Saviour, who had rescued him from darkness all those years ago.

(4) Final Trials: 'All is Well'

Although Simpson was heavily engaged in preaching the gospel and in caring for his congregation, he never neglected his domestic duties. His household assembled every morning and evening for worship, and each member was given an opportunity to take part. He taught his children to read 'properly, distinctly and gracefully'; to 'love their Bible above all other books, and God above all other beings'; and urged them to 'aim at excelling in the most trifling matters'. They were warned against keeping bad company; encouraged to be 'lively, cheerful and affectionate; to strive to please and be pleased'; to avoid 'absence in conversation', to 'take reproof well', to be 'prudent, cautious and discreet', and to take care of their health, since they only had 'one life to lose'.[1] His daughters were 'taught the languages', but in order to restrain pride, 'not to discover that they knew anything about them, unless upon very particular occasions'.

There are many letters that illustrate the affection and concern he had for his children's physical and spiritual well-being. In a letter to his daughter, he wrote,

How swift and imperceptible is the flight of time! Five weeks are gone since you left us, and they appear but so many days. The same will be our reflection at the close of life itself! How parsimonious should we be of every moment, on the proper improvement of which hang *everlasting* things! How imprudent are we to squander every day, with profusion, many of those moments we shall be glad, ere long, to purchase at the price of worlds, if we had them! You remember the dying words of Salmatius, who was unquestionably one of the first scholars that ever lived: 'Oh! I have lost a world of time! of time, the most precious thing in the world! whereof had I but one year more, it should all be spent in David's Psalms, and Paul's Epistles!' What a lesson ought this to be to us![2]

All his correspondence with his family was of the same character, full of love to God and others, saturated with a deep humility that thought nothing of himself and everything of his Saviour, and inspired by an honest desire to serve his Master with the 'little strength' he possessed. In a letter to his second wife, Elizabeth Davey, a Methodist whom he married in October 1776 (they had three children, one of whom died on 5 December 1783 aged fourteen weeks), he wrote,

How strangely do I dream life away! Surely I am one of the greatest fools in nature! Blessed and chastened, and yet a fragrant rebel still! O that I might begin to live wholly to the Lord, who redeemed me.

I wish to live only to God, and for him, and to exhaust all the little strength I have in his service. True it is, I am the lowest, poorest, meanest of all my Master's heralds; but I am not weary of that service, but would hold the candle, or scrape the shoes of any of his servants that I judge are such, in sincerity and truth.[3]

According to popular testimony, Elizabeth cared for her stepdaughter, who after the death of David's first wife had been looked after by his sister-in-law, 'with an affection and solicitude rarely equalled'.

Simpson's health was at times fragile, with symptoms of paralysis occasionally occurring. Richard Reece, who knew Simpson for the last eighteen months of his life, said,

I became acquainted with him in August 1797, when he had the appearance of vigorous health; and frequently from the pulpit heard him announce the *word of reconciliation* to perishing sinners, with a warmth of zeal, and plainness of language, I had never, till then, heard in the church. But though he had the flush of health, I soon found that his ardent labours had greatly impaired his constitution; and that after the toils of the Sabbath he was frequently unwell for a day or two. Notwithstanding, at those times he had always some publication in hand, calculated to serve mankind.[4]

About nine months before his death Simpson wrote to a friend, saying, 'My own complaint is my old companion, my head, which makes bad work with me at times, and always is injurious to my memory and my usefulness. I sometimes think it will leave me an idiot. Lately I have had five strokes of the palsy, which took away the use of my left side, and half of my tongue.'[5] On 5 July 1798, he wrote to his brother-in-law, Mr Myles, and gave further details of this attack and his subsequent recovery. 'A few weeks ago, I was taken all down my left side with a stroke of the palsy, as I was talking to a poor man in my study. It returned five times. At present, with the blessing of God upon the means, I am pretty well recovered, and have been only laid by one Sabbath Day.'[6] In the same letter he unveils some of his 'homely' thoughts.

I love you all as affectionately as ever I did, and frequently both think of you, talk of you, and pray for you, and sometimes even dream of you. My mind, when I wake and when I sleep, makes many an excursion into my dear native place, which, notwithstanding the homeliness of it, I prefer to every other spot upon the globe; and, if divine providence should so order it, I would rather settle among you, in some small sequestered spot, with a few kind friends, than be promoted to the first living, or even to the best bishopric in the kingdom. These are not words of course, but the genuine dictates of my mind. Honour and popularity have lost their charms with me, and I only long for more of the mind that was in Christ; for the sensible, heartfelt, experimental consolations of his religion, and for a meekness to enter into the society of just men made perfect.[7]

The sentiments about 'my dear native place' are echoed in an earlier letter.

I often feel a wish to spend the last part of my life in my native neighbourhood, in preaching the gospel from village to village. Nor am I without hopes that one day this may be the case. If providence should call me, I cheerfully would obey. My heart yearns over various parts of my native country. Some years ago I felt the same drawing towards a certain destitute village. I went and preached to the inhabitants twice at their doors. A place of worship was built, and now they are favoured with a regular ministry.[8]

Soon after he wrote the letter to his brother-in-law, Simpson and his wife were deeply grieved when their only daughter Elizabeth died of 'a consumption' on 25 July 1798, just a few months before their own deaths. She was only eighteen. In an interesting letter to a 'dear brother', Simpson expresses hope that she belonged to Christ.

My dear brother,

I have now to inform you, that my dear Betsy took her leave of mortal things on the 25th of last month, at eight o'clock in the evening, after a severe affliction of five months, during the whole of which time, she was patient and resigned, beyond what I have almost ever seen or known. Towards the latter part of her illness, however, she was much more than resigned; she was all on the stretch for mercy and salvation. You may be sure it has been a severe trial to her mother and myself, and the more so, as we are now left childless at home [by this time their third child, David, had moved to London], and as she was the only daughter of her mother.

It has been a time of much fatigue to Mrs Simpson, because she scarcely ever could be prevailed upon to leave our poor dear child by day, and never by night, for all the five months. She is, however, pretty well, thank God, and bears our loss with remarkable fortitude and firmness of mind. Indeed, we have much reason to be both resigned and thankful, because we have no reason to sorrow as those who have no hope.

I am, my dear brother,

Yours affectionately,

D. S.[9]

Mrs Simpson's dedicated caring for her sick daughter and subsequent bereavement weakened her own constitution. Medicine and a change of air were tried, but without effect. Within a short time her condition deteriorated so drastically that she was unable to walk to church without help, and then she had to be carried to communion in a sedan chair. Eventually she was unable to go outside at all. On 27 February 1799, Doctor Howard of Knutsford was called, and he immediately announced that she was seriously ill. Her submissive response was to cry, 'God is faithful, and has promised never to forsake them that trust in him.' From that time she gave up all desire to live and requested that the things of this world might not be mentioned to her. She knew she was going to die and wanted to be ready for her final hour; but on 7 March the devil tempted her to doubt the promises of God, and for a while she felt despondent, her soul refusing to be comforted. She thought she had deceived herself, that she had been in a deep sleep all her life and was just now waking up to a sense of her misery. The next morning, however, in answer to fervent prayers, the Lord strengthened her with his love, and she finally rested in the joyful assurance of God's unchangeable promise of salvation.

From the time of her deliverance, prayer and praise were continually on her lips and the tempter was no longer able to afflict her. On 10 March, three days before her death, she was happy and at peace, and after spending the day in prayer, she exclaimed with peculiar vigour,

Give me a place at thy saints' feet,
Or some fall'n angel's vacant seat;
I'll strive to sing as loud as they,
Who sit above in brighter day.

She was delirious for the next two days, during which time her husband wrote an affecting letter to their son David, of Bishopsgate Street, London.

My dear Son,

Your mother and I have both been confined to our beds for above a fortnight. I can hardly tell you what my complaint is, but I am brought very low. Your mother's complaint is a fever of the most dreadful kind. Her fate must be decided for life or death in two or three days. I would not have you come over till you hear from me again, which shall be by tomorrow's post, God willing. If you were upon the spot, you could have no communication with her, nor even be permitted to see her, as she is generally delirious. The Lord bless you, my dear son. You shall hear again tomorrow.

Your affectionate,

But deeply afflicted father,

DAVID SIMPSON.[10]

On the morning of the 13th Mrs Simpson regained her senses and spent a few hours in prayer and praise. At six o'clock she fell into a deep sleep, and an hour later she slipped quietly into the presence of her Saviour. She was fifty-six.

Elizabeth had been a perfect soul mate for her husband, supportive of his ministry and a godly woman in her own right. Her manuscripts, written only for private use, 'show such a measure of godly fear, such a dedication to the divine glory, such a concern for the salvation of others, especially her children, as stands associated only with *eminent* piety'.[11] A few weeks before her death, she wrote the following lines, indicative of her deep personal faith.

Oh, thou blessed God! Thou art, when every creature fails, a never-failing friend. Blessed be thy holy name, I have found thee ever faithful (though I am most unfaithful); ever faithful to thy *promise*. Thou hast promised—as thy day so shall thy strength be. Thou hast, in a particular manner, fulfilled this promise to me the last year. I pray thee,

O Lord, to help me to look upon myself as a stranger and a sojourner here, in this vain, unsatisfying world. O help me, enable me, I pray thee, for if thou dost *not*, my heart will be for cleaving to something here below. But, oh, I would not. I wish to sit loose to everything. Let me have fellowship with thee, thou ever-blessed Jehovah—Father, Son and Spirit.[12]

Her practice had been to take the female servants into her bedroom every afternoon for a time of prayer. On Thursday evenings she assembled her children and any young visitors for religious instruction. She sang, prayed and talked with them of religious matters in a most engaging manner, and each young person repeated his or her accustomed form of prayer. One member of that party, after he had grown up, became a man of considerable fortune and an occasional preacher in Wesley's connexion. On at least one occasion he gratefully acknowledged his debt to Mrs Simpson, and 'expressed his earnest wish that every domestic circle might be favoured with as equally effective course of religious training'.[13]

Soon after the start of his wife's sickness Simpson himself was taken ill with 'malignant typhus'. At the time Macclesfield was enduring an outbreak of fever and Simpson caught the disease while visiting a poor sick family who lived on the common near the town. Before long a bad cough and high temperature incapacitated him. To make matters worse, he felt distraught that he was unable to help his wife, who lay in an adjoining room. He only *heard* of her holy joy and peaceful end. However, he rejoiced in the firmness of her faith and the goodness of God towards them both. The 'paralytic affections', with which he had been afflicted for some time, returned so frequently and impaired his health so badly that he knew his work as a minister was almost over. He did not preach for the last six weeks of his life.

During the time of his suffering he turned to his son-in-law, John Lee, who had married his daughter by his first marriage, and spoke with affection and confidence. 'I am quite *satisfied* with all the dispensations of providence, though they may appear to be severe—very severe—but I am quite *satisfied* … All *is* well—all *shall* be well; and it is right and just. I have every reason to praise him.'[14] At times, when he was overly anxious about his wife, he turned his eyes to the Lord. 'God is going to close up the scene at once, and end our lives and labours together. It is an awful Providence, but it is His will, and I have no desire to return again to health.'¹⁵ Speaking of his *Plea for Religion*, he said, 'I have no doubt but my motives have been such as the Almighty approves, and I leave the whole to him.'¹⁶

On Saturday 16 March, he was 'very poorly'. Lee expressed a hope of his recovery, to which he replied, 'No, I shall never get better in this life. I have no desire to come back to life. I am tired of this life; tired of its vanities, tired of its follies, tired of its amusements, tired of its business. My work is done. I leave the great scene of things now passing in the world to you. Why should I wish to live?'¹⁷ On another day he asked for some hymns to be read to him, one of which was *Jesus, lover of my soul*. He remarked how that hymn had comforted many others in similar circumstances, as well as himself. He dwelt on the verse 'other refuge have I none' and said, 'This is true of me. What a poor creature I am!'¹⁸

All his hope and confidence were in God, and he was frequently supported by the words of Scripture. The next day he asked Lee to read to him. Lee picked up a hymn book, but was stopped. 'I want some comfortable portion from the *blessed Scriptures*; all human support now fails me. Read some comfortable portion.' Lee read: 'When my flesh and heart fail me, God is the strength of my heart, and my portion for ever.' In reply he acknowledged that passages like the one read frequently occurred to his mind and supported him, before adding, 'I am not dying as one who has no hope; very far from it. I consider all my eternal concerns as *settled*. All my dependence rests upon the great atonement. I have committed all my concerns into the hands of my Redeemer.' He then turned to his friend Peter and asked him, 'Tell the people I am not dying as a man without hope,' and expressed his strong assurance of the happiness that awaited him.

In the evening he said solemnly, 'This is a very serious dispensation. It appears severe, very severe; first the shepherdess is taken away, and then the shepherd, and both as by one stroke. But I am perfectly *satisfied* respecting it; and this our light affliction, which is but for a moment, shall work out for us a far more exceeding, and an eternal weight of glory.'¹⁹

As his condition worsened, his flock joined together in prayer for his restoration, as well as people in other places of worship in the town, but it was not God's will. According to a letter written by Lee at the time, he 'would, if it were possible, fly on the wings of a seraph; he wants only a seraph's tongue to sing the praises of his Redeemer as loud as they. We have, therefore, here in the midst of our tribulation, a little heaven.'[20] After a severe coughing fit, he called to his attendant, 'The way seems hard, but it is the way the children of God all go, and I do not wish to be exempted from it. I know that my Redeemer liveth. I feel him precious to my soul. He supports me under all. O that I could express all I feel!' When the doctor arrived and asked him how he was, he replied, 'Partly here, and partly elsewhere.'[21]

On another occasion he cried out to the person who was with him, 'How awful a thing it is for a man to be brought to his dying bed, and to have no hope beyond the grave. It is truly awful; but, blessed be God, this is not my case.' To his curate he uttered, 'To me, to live has been Christ, and to die will be gain.'[22]

On Tuesday morning, 19 March, he addressed his son, who had returned from London, and with great affection said, 'I hope the Lord will bless you when I am gone. I trust he will; and I commend you to the word of his grace, which is able to build you up, and to give you an inheritance among all them which are sanctified. The Lord bless you, the Lord bless you.' To Lee he said in the kindest manner, 'Farewell, my dear son. God bless you—God bless you.' As his strength rapidly declined he often imagined himself to be preaching to his congregation. He spoke much of the glories of heaven and the happiness of separate spirits, of their robes of righteousness and palms of victory, adding, 'Pardon, peace and everlasting salvation are desirable things.'[23] Sometimes he ministered to his fellow clergy who visited him, warning them to be good stewards. 'Men and brethren,' he said, 'if you are called of God—are faithful and honest, he will bless your labours!' But he could not continue talking in that strain for long.[24]

Nine days earlier he had asked Reece, 'When is Lady Day?' Reece had replied, 'Monday, the 25th.' 'I shall be gone before then,' Simpson had responded, and so it proved. Just before midnight on 24 March 1799, after a day of apparent suffering, he was released from this life of toil and hardships, and welcomed into his eternal home. Thus, after an active and

*Simpson's mural monument, which consists of a
representation in Basso Relievo of the good Samaritan*

fruitful pilgrimage, twenty-seven years of which were spent in Macclesfield, this servant of God aged fifty-four finished his course and received his reward.

His funeral the following Tuesday was attended by an 'immense multitude', and several persons walked in solemn procession in front of the coffin singing hymns, while the bells of both churches tolled in lament. His remains were interred 'amidst the sighs, and groans and tears' of many, including children, in a vault outside Christ Church, where he had been used so effectively. The service in the church, which contained near to three thousand people, and particularly the address, were the means of the 'powerful re-awakening of the early religious impressions' of James Townley, who had been educated when young by Simpson. Townley, who in 1827 was appointed one of the General Secretaries of the Wesleyan Missionary Society, frequently spoke of the occasion, and usually with deep emotion.

Many sermons were preached in affectionate tribute to Simpson, including one by Coke in Manchester's Oldham Street Chapel from 2 Samuel 3:38: 'Know ye not that there is a prince and a great man fallen this day in Israel.' Joseph Nightingale, a Wesleyan Methodist, published *Elegiac Thoughts, occasioned by the death of the Rev. D. Simpson*, to which were added short extracts from Simpson's most approved publications; a Methodist preacher wrote an elegy in which he highlighted Simpson's stand for the truth and benevolent causes; and the periodicals, both newspapers and magazines, abounded with notices of his distinguished labours and death. Hatton, the rector of Waters Upton in Shropshire, in a letter of condolence to the family, called Simpson a 'burning and shining light'. 'He is now reaping the fruits of his labours in a blessed eternity; he has received the approbation of his Redeemer, and been welcomed with that ravishing salutation: "Well done, good and faithful servant, enter thou into the joy of thy Lord!"'[25]

In Christ Church, Macclesfield, a monument was erected to his memory 'by an affectionate people, as a grateful acknowledgement of the benefits they had derived' from their pastor's ministry. It bears the following inscription:

SACRED to the Memory
of the Revd DAVID SIMPSON, M.A.
the first Minister of this *Church*,
Who, after 24 years Laborious & unremitted Service,
departed this Life, March 24, 1799,
Aged 54.

As a preacher of the *Gospel* he was zealous and faithful;
Pure and uncorrupt in his doctrine;
A pattern of good works in his Life;
A Friend to the poor and distressed;
A Comforter of the Sick and afflicted;
A Father to the Orphan;
A Husband to the Widow;
And confining his benevolence neither to Sect or Persuasion,
He was in his Universal *Charity*,
THE GOOD SAMARITAN.[26]

Another epitaph, originally designed for a pane of glass, included the following sentiments:

THE REV. DAVID SIMPSON. A.M.
For extent of erudition,
Indefatigable diligence,
Ardent zeal, and amenity of manners,
Stood unrivalled ...
Many, whom he found brutes,
He left Christians.
His pious care, like that of his
GREAT MASTER,
Extended to the bodies of the poor of his flock;
The abodes of hopeless anguish he sought out,
And to administer medicine
For the relief of affliction,
Was his uniform practice for many years.[27]

It has been said that his 'whole life was a beautiful illustration of the religion to which he was devoted'. John Gaulter and James Johnson have left these fitting tributes to him:

His mind classed among the most vigorous and acute. His reading was as extensive, as his application was incessant. His study was not the region of gratification, so much as of improvement; and his accumulated store of Biblical erudition, was directed more to the experimental and practical branches of religion, than to critical nicety, or the elaborate culture of the higher ornaments of language. His reading of the public service of the church was graceful and correct. In the pulpit, his discourses were generally plain, and delivered with great, but inartificial fervour. Affecting not the chaste art of modern address, yet equally remote from vulgarity; to use Mr Baxter's words, he preached as a dying man to dying men. In personal holiness and labours he left but few equals, and on his death the general sentiment was,

> 'He was a man, take him for all in all,
> 'We ne'er shall look upon his like again.'[28]

The remarkable success that attended his ministry is not difficult to account for. It was the result, under God, of the experimental character of his preaching; of the stability that enabled him to live down prejudice; the zeal which he expended upon the education of the young; the philanthropy which led him to seek the bodily comfort as well as the spiritual welfare of those around him; and the largeness of heart which caused him to cooperate in well-doing with good men from whom he differed on minor points. Each of these causes contributed in its degree to the extraordinary influence he acquired … David Simpson ought to be considered, without doubt, one of the great ones in the kingdom of heaven.[29]

*   *   *   *

For some time before his death Simpson had carefully considered his position in the Church of England, and whether or not he should leave to join the dissenters. Various factors were involved in his decision: the way he had been treated by members of the Establishment, his activity and zeal for the gospel, frowned upon by many in the Church; his belief in catholicism before canonical restrictions and exclusiveness (he was opposed to any system that curtailed the full proclamation of Christ); and Episcopal refusal to allow his good friend John Wesley to preach in his church. In other words, it was his forthright Protestantism—by that we mean that whatever claimed his faith and affections, he examined carefully in the light of Scripture—that finally persuaded him to leave the Establishment.

Many in the Church of England tried to dissuade him from taking what they regarded as a 'grave step that would cause irrevocable harm'. Even some men connected with Wesley, who would have gained by his friend's defection, resisted his planned departure from the Church. Alexander Mather, one of Wesley's eminent fellow-workers, wrote to Simpson, urging him to retain his ministerial position.

None would be more glad than I to see Mr Simpson in our Connexion, if I did not know, (1) that the present was the appointment of God; (2) that your loss to the Church would be such as could not be balanced by any gain to the Methodists, even in the fullest use of your very extraordinary talents in their favour. (3) I am more confident you could not endure the fatigues of an itinerant life, to say nothing of Mrs Simpson's health: no, not if it were in our power to make every provision for you both, that my heart could prompt to; and this I know it is not, as we are now circumstanced.[30]

All such pleadings were to no avail, for Simpson planned to make his decision public in the appendices of a new edition of *A Plea for Religion*, originally published in 1797, but twelve hours before it was released he died. His comments were then withdrawn.

The advertisement of the 1802 edition of the *Plea*, which contains the appendices, states that Simpson's executors 'hesitated on the propriety of making [his decision] public', but that his son, David, 'thought it his duty to perform the intentions of his father'.[31] John Williams remarks that Simpson's 'apology' 'evinces, not only a brilliant specimen of conscientious self-denial and intrepid firmness, but the courage of a noble soul—the decision, after deep reflection, of a thoroughly honest man'.[32] Some of the clergy were immediately alienated by the publication, while others denounced it with bitterness and poured on the author, 'though dead, a redundance of abuse', branding him 'disloyal'.

It is not our intention to comment at any length on the appendices, only to say that his criticisms of the clergy unveil his own zeal for the gospel and, sadly, present the reader with a vivid picture of the eighteenth century Church. His desire was to see a thorough reformation within the Establishment.

Whatever militates against the genuine spirit of Christ's religion in the establishment should be removed; and that all orders of clerical characters, especially, should set themselves, with the utmost zeal and determination, first to reform themselves, and then to stop the torrent of iniquity, which threatens to involve the country in the most complete destruction. The Dissenters and Methodists are moving heaven and earth to promote the cause of religion in their respective ways. If the 18,000 clergymen in the establishment would exert themselves for the good of souls with equal zeal and fervour, the Established Church would not only be the safer, as an Establishment, but the divine protection would be more effectually engaged on our behalf … Unfortunately, however, abundance of our order of men are the greatest enemies the country and religion have got. We promote the interest of Satan more effectually by our indolence, worldly-mindedness, lukewarmness, and misconduct, than all the wicked and immoral characters in the kingdom put together.

He then imagines the 18,000 clergy, led by 26 bishops, all filled with faith and the Holy Spirit, with an ardent love for Christ and a zeal for the salvation of souls, sent to all the corners of the land to preach the everlasting gospel. 'What a glorious consideration!'

He wants there to be a new unity of purpose in the churches. 'We ought every one to step out of the routine of our accustomed methods of doing good, and strive, with a peculiar energy, to save our people's souls from death, and our beloved country from ruin.' He notices how the Methodists 'are much more upon the increase than we of the Establishment, who are fostered by the government, attended by the nobles and gentry of the land, and supported by the state, at the expense of near two millions a year'. The 30,000 villages in England cry out 'for every exertion to evangelise them, and to save the people's souls alive'. He cites the example of the Methodists, who reach people far and wide, and then exclaims,

Shall we … of the Establishment … be all asleep, sit still and pursue no peculiarly vigorous measures, each one in our own sphere, or various of us in concert, till destruction come upon us to the uttermost? … Let the very laudable conduct of the several zealous bodies of Christians in this nation … not excite our rage and envy, but rather let it provoke the great body of us, the established clergy, to jealousy and emulation. [Let] the archbishops and bishops … come among their clergy and people, and set us an example of a warm and judicious zeal in preaching … the great and glorious truths of the everlasting Gospel … This would have a strong tendency to animate and encourage the pious part of the clergy in their ministerial labours for the good of mankind, and to discountenance and overawe the licentious and profane, those dreadful pests of every neighbourhood which has the misfortune to be cursed with their example.

At present most of the bishops and clergy are a 'useless burden upon the public'.

While we continue dead to the interests of religion—subscribe what we do not believe—read what we do not approve—and set the pulpit and reading desk at loggerheads one with the other; while our doctrines are unevangelical—our spirit lukewarm—our minds secular and worldly—our studies literary or philosophical— and our conduct immoral; far better would it be that the nation were without us, and all our preferments sequestered to the purposes of the state as they respectively become vacant, and the people left to provide at their own expense for ministers, as it is among all denominations of Dissenters.

He criticises the overpayment of bishops and clergymen, regarding clergy with large preferments as 'the drones of society. They neither write anything to good purpose, nor do they take any serious pains in their vocation of preaching the Gospel … Not being truly in earnest for their own salvation, they have but little zeal for the salvation of others.'

With all that Simpson said in the first appendix, it is not surprising that he should begin the second by saying, 'I do not see how I can, either in honour or conscience, continue to officiate any longer as a minister of the Gospel in the Establishment of my native country.' He saw the Church of England as 'a main branch of the *anti-christian* system. It is a strange mixture … of what is secular and what is spiritual.' He suspected that sooner rather than later 'the whole fabric shall tumble into ruins' and as a result the 'pure and immortal religion of the Son of God' will 'rise more bright, lovely and glorious'. In obedience to the injunctions of Scripture, such as Jeremiah 51:6,9, Matthew 24:15,16 and Revelation 18:4, 'and under a strong disapprobation of the several *anti-christian* circumstances of our own Established Church, *the general doctrines of which I very much approve and admire*, I now, therefore, withdraw; and renounce a situation, which, in some respects, has been extremely eligible. I cast myself again upon the bosom of a gracious providence, which has provided for me all my life long.'

In taking this extraordinary step he was obeying the dictates of his conscience, although that did not diminish the personal pain and anguish he experienced.

I am truly sorry for it. To me few trials were ever equal. I have loved the people among whom I have so long lived and laboured. And I have every reason to be satisfied with their conduct towards me ... The appearance of fruit, at times, has been large ... My friends must consider me as called away by an imperious Providence; and I trust they will be provided with a successor more than equal, in every respect, to their late affectionate pastor ... The doctrines which I have preached unto them for six-and-twenty years, I still consider as the truths of God ... I mean to preach the same doctrines, the Lord being my helper, during the whole remainder of my life ... I am not weary of the work of the sacred ministry. I have, indeed, often been weary in it, but never of it. I pray God my spiritual vigour, life and power and love and usefulness may abound more and more to the end of my Christian warfare.

In the rest of the paper Simpson answers anticipated objections to his departure and again reiterates that he is obeying 'the painful dictates of my own mind ... and conscience'. He knows the hurt his determination will give his 'dear people', but he must submit to the Head of the Church and endeavour to conduct himself agreeably to his pleasure. 'After a thousand defects, both in my public ministrations and private conduct, I can almost say, I have done my best to promote as well the temporal, as spiritual interests of the town of Macclesfield.' He closes by repeating the battle he endured in coming to his decision.

I have thought much upon the subject; read on both sides of the question whatever has fallen in my way; conversed with various persons for the sake of information; suffered the matter to rest upon my mind for some years undetermined; have never made my fears, suspicions and dissatisfaction known to any man; and now, when I bring near to myself the thought of quitting one of the most commodious churches in the kingdom, erected on purpose for my own ministrations; leaving interred by it many a precious deposit … besides a mother, a wife, two children, and a sister; and giving up various kind friends … together with a large body of people … What shall I say?—All that is affectionate within me recoils. I am torn with conflicting passions …

Various passages of Scripture … urge me … to renounce a situation which I cannot any longer retain with peace of mind … I bewail it exceedingly. I have received no affront, conceived no disgust; formed no plans; made no connexions; consulted no friends; experienced no weariness of the ministerial office; the ways of religion are still pleasant; I have been glad when duty called me to the house of God; his word has been delightful; the pulpit has been awfully pleasing: the table of the Lord has been the joy of my heart; and now that Providence calls me away, with some degree of reluctance it is that I say, Lord, here I am; do with me what seems good to you. Let me stay where I am. I gladly stay. Send me where you will. I will endeavour to submit. Only go with me, and your pleasure shall be mine.33

Perhaps the most appropriate closing comment is to remind the reader that Simpson's determination, whether right or wrong, was never carried through. The curtain of his life was drawn before he could preach on a different stage.

Endnotes

(1) EARLY YEARS: PREPARING FOR THE FIGHT OF FAITH

1 **David Simpson,** A Key to the Prophecies (London, William Walker & Sons, n.d.), p. 5.

2 **Sydney H. Moore,** 'A Quaint Hymnbook' in Congregational Quarterly, October 1951: p. 349.

3 **David Simpson,** A Plea for Religion and the Sacred Writings (Liverpool, Nuttall, Fisher & Dixon, 1812), p. 3.

4 **David Simpson,** A Plea for Religion and the Sacred Writings (London, Jackson & Walford, 1837), p. lxi.

5 **Alfred Leedes Hunt,** *David Simpson and the Evangelical Revival* (London, Chas. J. Thynne & Jarvis, Ltd, 1927), p. 21.

6 *Ibid.,* p. 18.

7 **Hunt,** *Simpson*, p. 13.

8 *Ibid.,* p. 15.

9 *Theological Tracts*, October 1791, pp. 237–238.

10 **Hunt,** *Simpson*, p. 26.

11 *Ibid.,* pp. 82–83.

12 **Simpson,** *Plea* (London, 1837), p. 264.

13 **Hunt,** *Simpson*, p. 106.

14 **David Simpson,** *A Plea for the Deity of Jesus and the Doctrine of the Trinity* (London, 1812), p. vi.

15 **Simpson,** *Plea* (London, 1837), p. iv.

16 **William Jones,** *Memoir of Rowland Hill* (London, Henry G. Bohn, 1853), p. 108.

17 *Ibid.,* p. 151.

18 **Hunt,** *Simpson*, p. 113.

19 **Edwin Sidney,** *Life of Rowland Hill* (London, 1861), p. 23.

20 **Simpson,** *Plea* (London, 1837), p. ix.

21 **David Simpson,** *A Plea for Religion and the Sacred Writings* (Philadelphia, 1809), p. iv.

22 **Simpson,** *Plea* (Liverpool, 1812), p. 6.

23 *Ibid.*

24 **Simpson,** *Plea* (London, 1837), pp. vi–vii.

25 **Sidney,** *Rowland Hill*, p. 61.

26 **Hunt,** *Simpson*, p. 18.

27 **Josiah Bull,** *But Now I See: The Life of John Newton* (Edinburgh, Banner of Truth Trust, 1998 reprint), p. 180.

28 **Simpson,** *Plea* (Liverpool, 1812), p. 8.

29 **Hunt,** *Simpson*, p. 172.

30 **William Goode,** *A Memoir of the Late W. Goode* (London, R.B. Seeley & W. Burnside, 1828), p. 8.

31 **Simpson,** *Plea* (London, 1837), p. xii.

32 **Hunt,** *Simpson*, p. 173.

33 *Ibid.,* p. 174.

34 **A.C.H. Seymour,** *The Life and Times of Selina Countess of Huntingdon* (Stoke-on-Trent, Tentmaker, 2000 reprint), vol. 2, p. 143.

35 **John Wesley,** *The Works of John Wesley* (Grand Rapids, Baker Book House, 1998 reprint), vol. 3, p. 190.

(2) MACCLESFIELD: THE BATTLE RAGES

1 **John Corry,** *The History of Macclesfield* (London, J. Ferguson, 1817), Appendix—Biography & p. 70.

2 **Simpson,** *Plea* (Philadelphia, 1809), pp. vi–vii.

3 **James Johnson,** *Memoir of the Rev. David Simpson* (Macclesfield, 1878), pp. 13–14.

4 **Hunt,** *Simpson*, p. 178.

5 *Ibid.,* p. 179.

6 **Simpson,** *Plea* (London, 1837), p. xiii.

7 **Johnson,** *Simpson*, p. 14.

8 **Corry,** *History of Macclesfield*, p. 134.

9 **Alexander Strachan,** *Recollections of the Life and Times of the Late Rev. George Lowe* (London, 1848), p. 163.

10 *Wesleyan-Methodist Magazine*, 1857, David Simpson and John Wesley, vol. 3, p. 896.

11 **Hunt,** *Simpson*, p. 191.

12 **David Simpson,** *Sermons on Useful and Important Subjects* (Macclesfield, T. Bayley, 1774), pp. 224, 226–227, 237–238.

13 **Simpson,** *Plea* (Liverpool, 1812), p. 9.

14 **Simpson,** *Sermons on Useful and Important Subjects*, pp. 47, 53, 73–74.

15 **Hunt,** *Simpson*, p. 221.

16 **Simpson,** *Plea* (London, 1837), p. xviii.

17 **Hunt,** *Simpson*, p. 221.

18 **Simpson,** *Plea* (London, 1837), p. xvii.

19 *Ibid.,* pp. xx–xxiii.

20 **Hunt,** *Simpson*, p. 229.

21 *Christian Observer*, 1841, p. 720.

22 **John Berridge,** *The Whole Works of the Rev. John Berridge* (London, 1864), pp. 529–530.

23 **B. Cliff,** *A Retrospect* (Macclesfield, 1875), p. 6.

24 **Corry,** *History of Macclesfield*, p. 128.

25 **Wesley,** *Works*, vol.4, p. 329.

26 **David Simpson,** *A Sermon* (Macclesfield, 1843), pp. 10–12, 14.

27 *Wesleyan-Methodist Magazine*, 1857, vol. 3, p. 897n.

28 **Simpson,** *A Sermon*, pp. 11–12.

29 Simpson, *Plea* (Liverpool, 1812), pp. 437–438.

30 Johnson, *Simpson*, p. 18.

31 *Ibid.,* pp. 18–19.

32 Simpson, *Plea* (London, 1837), pp. xiv–xv.

33 Simpson, *Plea* (Liverpool, 1812), p. 10.

34 *Ibid.*

35 Simpson, *A Plea for the Deity of Jesus*, p. xvi.

36 *Ibid.,* pp. xvi–xvii.

(3) MACCLESFIELD: YEARS OF TRIUMPH

1 Simpson, *Plea* (Liverpool, 1812), p. xvii.

2 Simpson, *Plea* (London, 1837), pp. 555–556.

3 Hunt, *Simpson*, p. 259.

4 *Congregational Quarterly*, October 1951, p. 353.

5 *Ibid.,* p. 350.

6 Johnson, *Simpson*, p. 23.

7 Corry, *History of Macclesfield*, p. 148.

8 Hunt, *Simpson*, p. 233.

9 Simpson, *Plea* (Liverpool, 1812), p. xx.

10 Cliff, *A Retrospect*, p. 8.

11 Corry, *History of Macclesfield*, p. 131.

12 Simpson, *Plea* (Liverpool, 1812), p. xix.

13 Johnson, *Simpson*, pp. 32–33.

14 Simpson, *Plea* (London, 1837), p. xxxv.

15 Luke Tyerman, *The Life and Times of John Wesley* (London, Hodder & Stoughton, 1890), vol. 3, p. 165.

16 Tim Brinton, *Original Letter*, Sunday 6 April 2003.

17 Wesley, *Works*, vol. 4, p. 95.

18 *Ibid.,* p. 223.

19 *Ibid.,* p. 413.

20 Hunt, *Simpson*, p. 238.

21 Simpson, *Plea* (London, 1837), p. lxiv.

22 Hunt, *Simpson*, p. 250.

23 Simpson, *Sermons on Useful and Important Subjects*, pp. 36–37.

24 Simpson, *Plea* (London, 1837), p. xxx.

Chapter 4

25 *Ibid.*, p. xxxi.

26 Hunt, *Simpson*, p. 248.

27 Simpson, *Plea* (London, 1837), p. xxxi.

28 Johnson, *Simpson*, p. 30.

29 Simpson, *Plea* (Philadelphia, 1809), p. xi.

30 Simpson, *A Key to the Prophecies*, p. x.

31 *An Elegy on the Death of the Rev. David Simpson.*

32 Brinton, *Original Letter*, Sunday 6 April 2003.

33 *Ibid.*

34 Hunt, *Simpson*, p. 247.

35 Simpson, *A Key to the Prophecies*, p. ix.

36 Hunt, *Simpson*, p. 262.

37 Simpson, *Plea* (Liverpool, 1812), p. xxxiv.

38 Hunt, *Simpson*, p. 261.

39 Simpson, *Plea* (London, 1837), p. xxviii.

40 *Ibid.*, p. xxix.

41 Hunt, *Simpson*, pp. 261–262.

42 Simpson, *A Key to the Prophecies*, p. xi.

43 Simpson, *Plea* (Liverpool, 1812), p. xxxiv.

44 Johnson, *Simpson*, p. 3n.

45 Hunt, *Simpson*, p. 261.

(4) FINAL TRIALS: 'ALL IS WELL'

1 Simpson, *Plea* (London, 1837), p. xli.

2 *Ibid.*, p. xlii.

3 *Ibid.*, p. xliii.

4 Simpson, *Plea* (Philadelphia, 1809), p. xii.

5 Hunt, *Simpson*, p. 244.

6 Simpson, *Plea*, (London, 1837), pp. xlvi–xlvii.

7 *Ibid.*, p. xlvii.

8 Hunt, *Simpson*, p. 242.

9 Simpson, *A Plea for the Deity of Jesus*, pp. xxvii–xxviii.

10 *Ibid.*, p. xxix.

11 Simpson, *Plea* (London, 1837), p. xlix.

12 *Ibid.*, pp. xlix–l.

13 *Ibid.,* p. l.

14 *Ibid.,* p. li.

15 Simpson, *Plea* (Philadelphia, 1809), p. xiii.

16 Simpson, *Plea* (Liverpool, 1812), pp. 12–13.

17 Simpson, *Plea* (London, 1837), p. lii.

18 Simpson, *Plea* (Philadelphia, 1809), p. xiv.

19 Simpson, *Plea* (London, 1837), p. liii.

20 *Ibid.,* p. liv.

21 Simpson, *Plea* (Philadelphia, 1809), p. xiv.

22 Simpson, *Plea* (London, 1837), p. liv.

23 Simpson, *Plea* (Philadelphia, 1809), p. xv.

24 *Ibid.*

25 Simpson, *Plea* (London, 1837), p. lvi.

26 From a photograph of the monument.

27 Simpson, *Plea* (Philadelphia, 1809), p. xvi.

28 Simpson, *Plea* (Liverpool, 1812), p. 14.

29 Johnson, *Simpson,* p. 35.

30 *Ibid.,* pp. 33–34.

31 Simpson, *Plea* (London, 1837), p. lix, n. 55.

32 *Ibid.,* p.lix.

33 Simpson, *Plea* (London, 1837), pp. 537–579.

Thomas Pentycross

Faithful to one cause

The history of the Christian church makes fascinating reading, especially how God takes ordinary and imperfect men, with obvious weaknesses, and uses them for his glory. Thomas Pentycross was just such a man. He was not exceptional in any particular field and could be indecisive and unclear in his thinking, and yet, despite his deficiencies, God equipped him to establish the gospel in the town of Wallingford and to lead many to a saving knowledge of Christ.

Pentycross was born in London on Boxing Day 1748. He was the only child of his father's second marriage. Both his parents were honest and reputable members of society, though in rather dependent circumstances. Little is known of his childhood, except that he was a bright and intelligent boy, who had a taste for learning. His father, recognising his talents, managed to secure a place for him at Christ's Hospital, where he made exceptional progress in the lower departments. He was soon admitted among the Grecians, all of whom were thought worthy to receive a university education, which ideally suited Pentycross, for from very early in life he had decided on a career in the Church.

His rapid advance in learning, his cheerful disposition and agreeable manners, soon earned him the respect of his tutors and fellow pupils. Making the most of his popularity, he succumbed to the natural levity of his heart. He was particularly fond of reading plays and other light and amusing pieces of literature, and would memorize his favourite passages. Then, with dazzling effect and dramatic skill, he recited them to the other boys, much to their enjoyment. In the summer months, very early in the morning, he assembled the boys of his ward, of which he was a monitor, and together they dressed each other up as actors in the best way they could from the clothes hanging in their wardrobes. Then, under the directorship of Pentycross, they performed those parts of the plays which most appealed to them. Apart from supervising the production, Pentycross always had the leading role, and as he was the 'Garrick' of the party, his spectacular performance won general

Thomas Pentycross

David Garrick (as Richard III), one of Pentycross's favourite actors

applause. One admirer of his poetical gifts and eloquence, even while he was still at school, was Sir Robert Walpole's son, Horatio, who found him 'very sensible, rational and learned' and who enjoyed corresponding with him. The Lord, however, had plans for him other than the histrionics of acting and the worldly glamour of the stage, for he soon directed his attention to the serious issues of life and death. A dissenting minister, who was then a boy in the same school and ward as Pentycross, although unable to account for the sudden and dramatic change in his companion's life, nevertheless relates the transformation and its immediate consequences:

These morning theatrical exhibitions had not continued long, before a sudden and evident change took place in the mind, the pleasures, and the conduct of the young Grecian. We had no more theatrical exhibitions; he no more spouted his favourite passages. He appeared now to be deeply impressed with eternal things. Coming myself out of a family reputedly Methodistical, and being at times under serious impressions, he soon attracted my notice, though younger than he; and I narrowly watched his motions and actions. Frequently, when walking up and down the front, and myself in the hinder part of the ward, I have heard him pour forth his soul; at times in pious ejaculations; and at others, in the most lively and ecstatic exclamations of joy and gratitude. Now, instead of diverting the boys as before, he often collected them around him, to instruct them in the things of God and religion. His conciliating manners soon reconciled them to the new system.

Horace Walpole, who admired Pentycross's poetical gifts and eloquence

As the Sabbath evening was a dull and leisure period to many boys, who had no book but their Bible to read, he took that opportunity especially, to assemble them together in a secluded place, and engaged them in prayer, singing, catechising, and expounding the holy Scriptures; and we believe he occasionally composed short sermons, which he read to them. Many of the boys were much gratified; and I hope some were profited.[1]

Pembroke College, Cambridge, where Pentycross met Rowland Hill

The dissenting minister notices how these religious exercises stirred up the prejudice and opposition of the matron of the ward. She had made no objection to Pentycross's theatrical performances, but as soon as he started to preach Christ, her enmity to the gospel was aroused. The affair became a serious dispute between her and the monitors. Eventually it was submitted to the steward, who, after thoroughly investigating the matter, decided that Pentycross should be allowed to continue with his religious activities. The boys were delighted, and their 'pastor' conducted his 'services' until he left school and went to university. In fact, so great was his influence for good on his fellow pupils that he obtained the nickname *Bishop*.

Sadly, just before he left school, and for some time afterwards, his heart grew cold and he drifted away from the things of God. He entered Pembroke College, Cambridge, where his attainments in Greek and Hebrew, and in mathematical studies, were considerable. In due course he obtained his degrees. Thankfully, while there, he became the close friend of Rowland Hill, whose

Rowland Hill, one of Pentycross's close friends

instruction and example were made instrumental in reviving past impressions, and in leading him into a clear and experimental acquaintance with the truths of the gospel. He was also on friendly terms with Charles de Coetlogon and David Simpson, and a few others who influenced him for good.

Hill gathered round him these like-minded friends and together they formed a 'club' similar to the 'Holy Club' at Oxford. They read the Greek Testament, expounded the Scriptures, joined in extempore prayer, attended 'unlawful' religious meetings, visited workhouses, sick rooms and inmates at the jail, and preached in the town and in the neighbouring area, calling sinners to repentance. 'As a result they brought down upon them a good deal of criticism, and even those members of the university who claimed to be religious held sternly aloof from them.'[2] Whitefield said of Pentycross at this time, 'Our dear Penty is under the cross at Cambridge.'[3] Irregularities such as these had caused the expulsion of six students from St Edmund Hall, Oxford, and so, because of their sensitive nature, several of his acquaintances advised him to desist, advice that he followed as he intended to be a regular and consistent member of the Church of England.

These 'Methodists' were also noted for having discovered the fire in Pembroke College in January 1768. The poet Thomas Gray, resident in the college, said, 'We owe it to Methodism that any part (at least of that wing) was preserved, for two saints [one of whom it is reasonable to suppose was Pentycross], who had been till very late at their nocturnal devotions and were just in bed, gave the first alarm.'[4]

During his college days Pentycross's ability and courage in defending the faith, brought one of the gownsmen to a serious concern for his everlasting welfare. This individual afterwards became a very popular preacher. Subsequently, when he fell away, Pentycross made repeated efforts to reclaim him and often poured out his soul in prayer to God for his restoration.

Thomas Gray

However, it seems that Pentycross became unsettled in his views and contemplated leaving the university and all prospects of orders, and going to the Welsh college Trevecca instead. In order to talk over his confusions and doubts he visited John Berridge at Everton, who later gave Whitefield an account of their meeting in his own inimitable style.

There is something very amiable in dear Penty. He came to my house about three weeks ago, and brought two pockets full of doubts and scruples relating to the Articles and Liturgy. I would fain have had the scruples left at Everton, but he took them all back with him to college, and seemed determined not to part with them. I believe the Lord loves him, and designs him for great things. Perhaps he may be intended for a spiritual comet, a field preacher like yourself; this seems to be his great aim and ambition. When he left me he talked of going to the Welsh College [Trevecca]. May the Lord direct him.[5]

At length he overcame his objections to taking orders, but, because of his evangelicalism, it was some time before he found a bishop willing to ordain him, probably not until 1771. On 1 August 1770, Rowland Hill, who was also suffering persecution for his faith, and rejoicing in it, wrote a lengthy letter of encouragement to Pentycross, drawing on his own experience. He urges his friend to consider working in Bristol.

My dear Penty,

I never sat down to write you with such a glee as at present, since I have known you. From the very bottom of my soul I wish you joy, on account of your being an outcast for God. This good news I had about nine days ago … I could scarce help writing to you immediately, but have, with much pain, waited till you could have this letter free. Your rejection pleases me so much the better, on account of your having met with it from my old friend, the prelate of York, who was the last, blessed be God, that put the same honour upon me.

At first, when they began to reject me, I was coward enough to give way to my fears, and fool enough to conclude that unless I went forth overlaid with black, the very colour of the devil, I never should prevail; but blessed be God that every day's experience more fully proves to me that all my fears were nothing but deceit.

Will my dear Penty (though he has frequently rebuked me for it) suffer me to boast myself a little; while I think I may venture to say, I mean it not for my glory, but for *your* encouragement …

Thousands and thousands attend all about these parts, and the evident power of great grace is abundantly amongst us. We have more than enough daily before our eyes, fully to convince us that no human garb, or human authority, shall ever be wanting, when the power of the gospel is present to heal. Upon the whole, every day's experience more fully satisfies me that all things have ever hitherto happened, have been entirely for the best.

I do not, however, my dear brother, mean to lay down my conduct as a rule for your walk; no, I trust, from my soul, that I detest the thought of ever assuming that place in any man's conscience, which so strictly belongs to God. My only and ardent prayer for you is, that God may abundantly baptize you with his Holy Spirit—first fit you for his will, and then teach you what it is. If your eye is but simple, and your heart indeed devoted to God, no doubt you will not long be left in the dark.

After having said this much, I mention what follows in general terms. As a despised outcast, and servant of the dear Lord Jesus, I can answer for hundreds, yea, I may say thousands, that long to have the honour to receive you, as a messenger of the gospel, in their open arms. I can answer for Bristol above all places besides—how gladly they would receive you, as their own soul! and as they have done me the unsought kindness to put me into the Tabernacle connexion in that city, and having thereby some right to send you an invitation, I do, with multitudes of others, send you a most cordial one; if you find your heart inclined to cast your despised lot amongst us, pray come without delay. The harvest in these parts is truly very great, and our labourers are but few.[6]

William Romaine, a friend, patron and supporter of Pentycross

There is no record as to whether

Pentycross accepted his friend's invitation, but the letter reveals that he was already a popular preacher among evangelical congregations.

His first appointment after ordination was to the curacy of Horley, near Reigate, Surrey, where he was patronized by William Romaine, for whom he occasionally officiated. At Horley the Lord blessed his ministry and numbers were converted. However, it was not long before his fervour and faithfulness to Christ and the gospel raised opposition.

On 23 January 1774, in his London chapel, he assisted John Wesley, who exclaimed, 'O what a curse upon the poor sons of men is the confusion of opinions! Worse by many degrees than the curse of Babel, the confusion of tongues. What but this could prevent this amiable young man from joining heart and hand with us?'[7] Early in the same year, the living of St Mary's, Wallingford, north west of Reading, became available, but, as it was worth only £12 a year, no clergyman in the area thought it worthwhile to accept. A member of the Methodist society in the town, recognising the usefulness of the opportunity, applied to Romaine, stating that Wallingford might be a good sphere for an evangelical minister, and promising that if Romaine could secure the services of one of his acquaintances, he would promote a subscription for his support and contribute liberally himself.

Romaine mentioned the matter to Pentycross, who in turn mentioned it to Lady Huntingdon. The countess 'strenuously urged' him to accept it, and as proof of her support, sent him £25, along with promises of her 'faithful intentions towards him, and earnest prayers for the success of his ministry'.[8] It did not take him long to obtain the living and he moved to Wallingford in the first half of 1774. A small subscription was started, but unfortunately the member of the Methodist society did not fulfil his promise. He declined to contribute, and in two or three years dropped the idea altogether, which inevitably left Pentycross in financial difficulties.

Wesley had first visited the town in

St Mary's, Wallingford

October 1769, and wrote enthusiastically in his *Journal*, 'How white are the fields here unto harvest! The whole town seemed flocking together, rich and poor, in the evening, and received the word with joy … Abundance of people came again at five in the morning, and were ready to devour the word. How pleasant it is to see the dawn of a work of grace!'9 A year later he mentioned a 'large and deeply serious' congregation at Wallingford, and in 1771 'many were moved' at his preaching. By 1777 a society had been formed.

However, despite Wesley's optimism from his fleeting visits, when Pentycross moved to Wallingford, the town was in a deplorable state of ignorance of Christ and open wickedness. There seemed to be little opportunity for good and little interest in the things of God. However, the new minister was not discouraged and set about tilling the barren land. He was in the prime of his life and in full possession of his faculties, and, with ardent zeal for the cause of Christ, he wielded the sword of the Spirit in the power of the Spirit. Before long the seed took root and started to grow, though there were numerous difficulties and many enemies ready to trample on the new crop.

To begin with there were only a few in the congregation, but soon the number began to grow, although he did not see the immediate increase he had anticipated, and therefore began to doubt his calling to Wallingford. He questioned whether the good seed of the kingdom had actually taken root and was tempted to quit his post. He did not want to make a hasty decision so he resolved to persevere for two or three years, and then to review the situation. On one occasion during this time, when he was away from Wallingford—perhaps he had taken time out to seek the Lord's will— a member of his congregation wrote to him, assuring him of the good work that was going on and the earnest desire of many of them for his return. This news was like water to a thirsty soul. With renewed zeal, redoubled affection for his flock, and thankfulness to God for shining a light on his path, he returned to Wallingford, determined to 'spend and be spent' for the good of his people. When he arrived, to his further delight, he discovered that many had been awakened to a sense of their sinfulness under his ministry.

In February 1775 Henry Venn, who was called from home to attend his mother-in-law's funeral at Highworth, Wiltshire, visited Wallingford on his journey, and enjoyed preaching to his friend's congregation. 'I stayed a day and a half at Wallingford, with Mr Pentycross. He is in a most useful sphere indeed, and has much favour with the people. I preached for him on Ash Wednesday. A most attentive congregation were present to hear; and, though I preached an hour and a half, not one seemed tired.'[10]

One young lady who had been converted through Pentycross's ministry was a Miss Allen, who lived in a neighbouring village. They became acquainted, fell in love, and were married in May 1775. Their relationship

Lady Huntingdon, a friend of Mr and Mrs Pentycross

was honouring to the Lord and they enjoyed many years of happiness together. Seymour says that in 'domestic life she was truly affectionate and pious, happily blending much good humour with unaffected seriousness'.[11] Lady Huntingdon always enjoyed her company, and in 1784, when Mrs Pentycross was in Bath for the benefit of her health, she received from the countess a silver teapot, accompanied by the following note:

Lady Huntingdon's kindest wishes ever attend Mrs Pentycross—was glad to find she was so well as to be able to arrive at her lodgings last night, though she fears she will feel the great difference in having left the hospitable roof of her kind friend, Mr Perry. A small token from Lady Huntingdon she hopes Mrs Pentycross will accept, to put her in mind how kindly she took her every remembrance of her when absence so justly might have left her so very excusable of every attention that could be due her. Lady Huntingdon hopes Mrs Pentycross will not suffer by the change of lodging; and as the air may be better, hopes they may both feel the best effects from it.

Bath, Feb.11, 1784.[12]

Soon after his appointment to Wallingford, and after supplying Lady

Huntingdon's chapel at Chichester for a few weeks, Pentycross travelled to Bath for the first time to visit the countess, who received him kindly and encouraged him in the work of the gospel. He was extremely grateful for her fellowship and advice, and returned to St Mary's full of the Holy Spirit.

To your ladyship [he wrote on his return] I am bound to yield unceasing thanks. Your counsels and your prayers have upheld me, have encouraged me, have stimulated me with a holy zeal, a vehement desire to spread the glories of Immanuel's name. O cease not to wrestle, with the great Angel of the Covenant, that I may be kept pure from the blood of all men—that no selfish passion mingle with my zeal, to corrupt the simplicity which is in Christ—but that I may be steadfast, unmoveable, always abounding in the work of the Lord—through every vicissitude of life conducting myself as a dying, accountable being, anticipating the awful period when the 'silver cord shall be loosed, when the dust shall return to the earth as it was, and my spirit to God who gave it'.

Your ladyship's mentioning my poor ministrations having proved acceptable, gives me courage and makes me confident of success.[13]

The serious hearers in his Wallingford congregation formed themselves into a compact group to encourage the heart of their minister and to give him all the support they could. Prayer meetings were established, where the godly poured out their souls to the Lord, and Pentycross himself preached with a deeper anointing. His fame began to spread in every direction and he was known as a 'Methodist *extraordinary*'. Many people from nearby villages came to hear him preach. Some came out of curiosity, to listen to a man so much talked about. Others came to ridicule a religious enthusiast, but many who came to *laugh*, returned home to *pray*. From one or two villages in particular, many families attended on a regular basis and sat under his ministry for several years. In order to accommodate them comfortably, he built another gallery in the church. Many others were soundly converted through the word he preached and their lives transformed, so that after his death, through Lady Huntingdon's Society, these families and their connexions were able to support a minister among themselves.

In the letter to Lady Huntingdon already quoted, he enthused about the success of the gospel:

Ever since my return to Wallingford I have been fully occupied in my ministerial labours. Glory be to God! The Sun of Righteousness has at length arisen, and shines upon this part of the vineyard. Let unbelief be confounded. If God will work, none can let it. How often has my wicked heart suggested that the Lord's time was not come, and how has this thought paralysed my exertions! But, oh! with what tenderness, what unparalleled affection has he reproved my vile ingratitude and unbelief! The light of divine truth has begun to dispel the awful gloom that hung upon this town and the surrounding neighbourhood, and many, lately sunk in ignorance and vice, now press to catch the cheering ray. The dews of heaven have descended on the seed of life, and it has taken root in many hearts. Now the wilderness and the solitary place is glad, the desert rejoices and blossoms as the rose, and this hitherto barren spot is converted into a pleasant field of fertility and joy.[14]

During this time of blessing, the enemies of the gospel were not idle. Opposition had arisen almost as soon as Pentycross arrived in Wallingford, but as the word spread and more lives were changed, so the vehemence and rancour of the opposition increased. Perhaps surprisingly, the chief opponent was the very man who had originally applied to Romaine for an evangelical minister! Various frivolous complaints were made against Pentycross to his diocesan, 'such as crowding the church, singing of hymns, speaking to the communicants at the sacrament'. The bishop repeatedly admonished him and eventually, as Pentycross refused to change his ways, summoned him to give an account of these irregularities.

Pentycross was represented by an eminent clerical friend, who spoke on his behalf to the bishop, who, after making a mild protest, allowed him to continue as he saw fit. This friendly interference was most providential, for Pentycross had not been unaffected by the opposition, some of which had been violent and sustained. At times his mind was perplexed and his spirit grieved, so much so that he was tempted to listen to proposals that would have led him to work in a different sphere, where he was highly respected and loved, and the Church would have lost one of its most useful ministers.

As the storm abated, Pentycross understood that the Lord wanted him to remain at his post in Wallingford, a decision that was confirmed in various ways. The joyful and triumphant deaths of some of his keenest supporters, alongside the awful deaths of others, who had strenuously opposed him, confirmed his resolve to stay. The man who had applied to Romaine was also sorely afflicted, and on many occasions begged for Pentycross's forgiveness and prayers, which he readily received. He too died prematurely. And so the antagonism towards him and his ministry subsided and he could continue his work in peace.

John Clayton, one of Pentycross's pupils

For some time he continued to struggle financially, and even with his wife's help, he never had enough to make ends meet; yet he was happy to serve God in poverty and to sacrifice his life for his beloved flock. At this juncture the way was opened for him to start a school, for which he was eminently qualified with his extensive learning and amiable personality. The undertaking was an almost immediate success. It not only enhanced his reputation, and thereby brought more people to Wallingford to hear the gospel, but eased his pecuniary difficulties, so that he was able to retire from it about three years before his death and live the remainder of his life in relative comfort.

Some of his pupils went on to respectable careers, and several ministers, both among the Church and the dissenters, were influenced by his example and received profitable instruction while under his care. John Clayton, the well known nonconformist minister, was one of his pupils, as was Thomas Marriott, the son of the noted Methodist philanthropist, William Marriott. When Thomas Marriott died in November 1852, he left £10 000 to the *Wesleyan Missionary Society* and the rest of his estate to the *Worn-out Preachers' Fund*. Pentycross was always ready to afford generous assistance to any promising young man, who desired to serve the Lord in the ministry.

He had first preached for Lady Huntingdon as early as 1765 at the opening of her chapel in Lewes. He also preached at the opening of her chapel in Chichester, and at Westminster and Bath. According to Seymour, he became a 'constant preacher' at her chapels, and maintained an 'intimate correspondence' with her until her death. In return she highly regarded his ministry, and his services were very acceptable and useful among her different congregations; indeed, says one, 'wherever he went, his talents and zeal, his eloquence and piety, commanded universal esteem'.[15] On one occasion, 'having enjoyed so many and great blessings' while in her company at Bath, he wrote to her from Wallingford with obvious affection and some adulation:

It would ill become me not to offer my unworthy services whenever your ladyship is pleased to command them. It will yield me unspeakable pleasure to be an humble instrument in furthering the plan you have in view for the promulgation of the glorious gospel of the ever-blessed God. Your embassy is an embassy of love; and should our great high priest smile upon your endeavours—still walk humbly with your God, and yield to him the entire glory of the work.

Into his everlasting arms I surrender your ladyship, with my utmost strength of faith and affection I honour your faith, which renounces abundance for poverty, and counts not ease or even life dear, so that you are the means of unfurling the banner of the cross and sending the glad tidings of salvation to people sunk in darkness, and covered with the shadow of death. May the smiles of him who dwells in Zion attend you in all your ways, and may his grace succeed you in bringing many sons to glory.

With many thanks, heartfelt thanks, for your many acts of kindness, I remain your grateful and very willing servant in the gospel of Christ,

THOMAS PENTYCROSS.[16]

In September and October 1782 Pentycross preached alternately with Thomas Wills at Bath, and their sermons were 'filled with solid good sense and well-digested sentiment, expressed in a style pleasing to the man of science, yet perfectly intelligible to the more illiterate, and were well calculated to inform the ignorant, to alarm the careless and secure, to comfort and edify the saint, and to make the sinner in Zion tremble'.[17] Lady Huntingdon paid tribute to their ministry, when she wrote, 'Dear Mr Wills and Mr Pentycross have left a mighty blessing behind them, in the many awakened and truly converted souls, the fruits of their honest labours among us. Blessed be God for such faithful men; O that he would send forth many, very many more *such* labourers into this plenteous harvest.' And again, when she wrote to Wills not long after his departure, 'It must comfort you … that you left a blessing behind you. Much rejoicing abides still with us, and dear Mr Pentycross keeps exceedingly alive in his own soul, and comforts the many, and causes fear to rest on the multitudes.'[18] In that same year, Pentycross preached Anne Walcot's funeral sermon at Lady Huntingdon's chapel in Bath from 1 Corinthians 15:56–57, which was afterwards published.

He obviously had no scruples about preaching abroad and labouring in other places. His desire was to preach Christ, whether among his own congregation, or elsewhere. He often preached for Rowland Hill at Surrey Chapel. Soon after the chapel was opened, Hill wrote to his friend David Simpson and said, 'Penty is now filling up my place in London; he grows greatly, and is by all accounts very lively in his ministry.'[19] During his visits he would 'look in upon the Sunday School'. 'Upon these occasions,' writes Hill in a letter from Wotton in 1786, 'he would look bigger than my lord bishop, threaten the disobedient with vast solemnity and egregious pomp, and applaud the well-behaved with that dignity of approbation that will make them the envy and admiration of all their schoolfellows.'[20] Once he met a worthy minister, for whom he had the utmost respect, and playfully engaged him in conversation. 'I have not forgotten my *sin* in having once given an exhortation at your place of worship.' His friend replied in a similar vein, 'I think it is a pardonable offence, and to prove it is forgiven, I should be happy to hear you repeat it.' From all accounts, however, the *sin* was not repeated.[21]

Although Pentycross enjoyed the blessing of God on his ministry from the outset of his time at Wallingford, there was one year that was particularly successful, the year 1783. Sunday after Sunday the presence of the Lord was felt in a tangible way and each week one or more members of his congregation were pierced to the heart, convinced of their sin, and led to the Saviour. Many in the town and neighbourhood, who had been unmoved previously, now felt and gladly acknowledged the power of efficacious grace. Pentycross delighted in this time of reaping and was both humbled and astonished at his success. Once he cried from the pulpit, 'The glorious year of seventeen hundred and eighty-three will never be forgotten by us through the ages of eternity!'[22] It was in 1783 that William Romaine preached at Wallingford[23] and no doubt delighted in what the Lord was doing.

After this period of blessing Pentycross was greatly admired by many and 'almost adored among his own people'. In some ways the success of the gospel in Wallingford tempted him to feel over-elated and proud of his achievements, taking too much of the credit himself. As a result he drifted, slowly but surely, from the purity of evangelical truth and started to indulge in the vain speculations of high Calvinism. In his preaching he disregarded the practical aspects of the truth and, unwittingly, fostered in his people a spirit of pride, self-conceit, stubbornness and an aversion to personal holiness.

In 1786, a dear friend, noticing the snare into which Pentycross had fallen, and with the best of motives, challenged his beliefs. Pentycross could not refute his friend's forceful arguments against the high notions he had adopted, and immediately saw their insinuating nature and the hindrance to the cause of holiness they naturally brought. In order to compensate for his error, he went to the opposite extreme and embraced some, though not all, of the Arminian or rather Baxterian opinions. With renewed zeal for the truth as he then understood it, and to counteract the Antinomianism he thought he had been teaching his flock, he laboured with boundless energy to urge his congregation to adopt his new system.

This sudden and unexpected change in his sentiments inevitably stirred up the high Calvinists. Some were grieved, others enraged, while the rest of the congregation was thrown into confusion. The heated arguments divided the church into two parties and eventually a separation took place. Those who left rejected their 'father in Christ' and sought to start anew. Although Pentycross was hurt by their actions, he was not one to hold grudges, and was always ready to take his share of the blame for what happened. Afterwards, when he was in the company of some friends in

London, one of them expressed regret that his people had behaved so ungratefully and in such an undutiful manner. Pentycross replied, 'How can I blame them, when I neither taught them their duty to God nor man? Preaching doctrine, doctrine perpetually, was the likely way to make them at length forget their duty to me.'[24]

Surprisingly, the separation was soon patronized by his friend Lady Huntingdon, who supplied preachers from her connexion. For the first year the separatists met in a private house, before they moved to a second house, in a more convenient location, which they converted into a chapel. It was opened in 1791 by Thomas Wills. However, even before the chapel was finished the seceders had argued among themselves and the newly formed congregation split, mainly because of a lawyer who had embraced antipaedobaptist sentiments. He built a chapel on his own estate and preached in it until his death in 1812. This second congregation was also patronized by her ladyship. Before long other changes and disputes arose between the groups, which prompted Pentycross to remark 'that schism was their sin, and schism would be their punishment'. What he predicted, he soon saw—'instability, impatience of control, party feuds, a frequent change of ministers, and other signs of an unfruitful profession'. Eventually matters settled down and, as the seceders gradually increased, two respectable congregations were formed.

This conflict between former members of his congregation grieved him deeply. If he did hear of any true prosperity among them, or that Christ was successfully preached, he rejoiced and gave thanks to God for his goodness. In fact, their progress in the gospel helped to reconcile him to the separation that had taken place, for he reasoned that if his successor at Wallingford was not an evangelical, his congregation could go to the dissenting meetings. His immediate successor was Edward Barry, who early in life had enjoyed the patronage of Lady Huntingdon, and been admitted to Trevecca in the hope that he would become one of her preachers. After he obtained orders and was inducted to the living of St Mary's, he turned against his former friends. A sermon he preached against them incited Seymour to highlight 'the theological errors, the defective morality, the misrepresentation of the inhabitants of Wallingford, the illiberality towards dissenters, and the antipathy and violence which are discoverable in this production'.[25] Another successor had been brought to a knowledge of the truth under Pentycross's own ministry.

After the separation, Pentycross made no attempt to regain those who had left, yet he soon saw the errors of Arminianism. In a letter to a dissenting friend, written some months after the separation, he voices his opinion on the seceders, and makes his doctrinal position clear.

Of the people who are withdrawn, several of them were turned out of my [private] society [which met at his house for spiritual instruction and devotion] first, for receiving *bribes* at elections; others are spouting Christians and rattlers. There are but few of them whom I esteem possessed of grace, or ever did, only I nursed appearances. The flower of my flock adhere to me, and are happier and more alive than ever. My congregations are larger, and my society more numerous than before; and the seceders are unattended to and forgotten. Their number amounts to about twenty.

I am not at all moved from the doctrines of free, sovereign, distinguishing, personal grace and election, but more *confirmed* in them than ever, on a thorough recent examination. Yet this I confess appears also to be true, that provision is made in Christ for all the world, and the only reason why any perish is because they will not come to him; as also, the only reason why any go to him, and get over the universal corruption and aversion to Christ is because miraculously and invincibly the Father draws them.

If the professing world reject this doctrine as Arminian, they know nothing of the opinions of the best Calvinist writers ... However, I profess myself of no party upon earth; neither Calvinist, Arminian, Baxterian, or anything else, but a Bible Christian ...

As to popular outcry, it proceeds from ignorance and misinformation. The method I hope to follow to suppress it is, to *outpreach, outpray and outlive it.* Here join me with your prayers; and believe me always, in the ever blessed *Jehovah our Righteousness,*

Your unworthy, most unworthy brother and friend,

T. PENTYCROSS.[26]

For a long while Pentycross was branded as an Arminian throughout the kingdom, a false accusation that was strengthened by a 'modern accuser of the brethren', who came to Wallingford at about this time. He saw fit to produce a slanderous two penny pamphlet entitled *Tidings from Wallingford*. To provoke Pentycross further, after he had been preaching to a crowded congregation at Surrey Chapel, his enemy had the gall to station some men at the doors to sell the pamphlets right under his nose. Pentycross made no reply to the accusations, nor would he allow a friend to finish the answer he had started. Instead, he prayed for and forgave the reviler.

After the clamour of these insults had died down, Pentycross continued faithfully in his parochial duties. Some of his former hearers returned to his church and became more attached to him than before, while many in his congregation judged that he 'now became, and ever after remained, a much more consistent, experimental, and scriptural preacher than before his lapse'. He blended the experience and holiness of the gospel with its doctrines, and, until near the close of his life, the Lord, in ones and twos, rescued people from the dominion of darkness through his preaching.

During this time John Wesley continued his sporadic ministry in Wallingford, with some success. In October 1787 he preached 'with much enlargement of heart', and Pentycross called upon him in the morning; in October 1788 he spoke to a 'serious and, it seemed, much-affected audience', and the following year 'to far more people than the preaching house could contain. It was a day of God's power, and I believe most of the stout-hearted trembled at his word.'[27]

Sometime during 1805 Pentycross gave up his school, though he was strongly urged to continue it. His desire, so he said, was to retire from the bustle of life and to prepare for death. Early in 1807 his health started to decline. In the autumn he tried the sea air, but received no benefit from it, and soon afterwards he lost his appetite and his strength; yet he continued his public ministry for as long as possible and spoke as one who knew he was standing on the edge of eternity. Three or four weeks before his death he wrote to his good friend, Rev. Marsh of Basildon, and in words of triumph, told him how he was feeling as his final hours approached.

I know not whether my Lord is sending for me home by this disorder; but he enables me to be found watching for that event. All my fears are banished away, and the most glorious hopes infused into me, by the most adorable Father, Saviour and Comforter.

I am one of the happiest of beings! though certainly, certainly, and *certainly* again, the most unworthy! Glory to God in the highest, for his love in giving us a Redeemer, and his Spirit to make that gift effectual! Hallelujah! Amen! And let all the universe say Amen! O let us glorify him in our souls and bodies in life, in death, and to eternity!

Tell everyone that heaven is free for them all, through the work and sorrows of Jesus Christ; if we want the true Saviour, one who renews as well as redeems, he is ours, and we are his. We cannot fail of eternal life, which God who cannot lie has promised in him before the world began. I am unable to proceed; my spirits flag.[28]

It was probably to the above letter that Thomas Scott, rector of Aston Sandford, Buckinghamshire, referred in his funeral sermon for Pentycross, taken from Hebrews 13:7–8, and published under the title *The Duty and Advantage of Remembering Deceased Ministers*. Scott remarked that the letter 'breathes a sweet spirit of confidence, gratitude, and admiring love; and a longing desire, that all did but know and experience his peculiar consolations and felicity. And as long as he could articulate, his discourse was in the same strain, and sometimes highly rapturous and triumphant.'[29]

The medication he was taking no longer helped him, and he gradually sunk, without much pain, into a lethargic state. He slept much and for most of the time was unable to talk with his friends. When he did speak, it was in the 'language of tranquillity, resignation and prayer'. Sometimes he was almost overcome with holy joy and rapture, and for the last two days of his life, though he spoke only rarely, he expressed his satisfaction and happiness. Finally, on 11 February 1808, he passed from this world of decay to the realms of eternal glory. He left behind a sorrowful wife, 'in the vale of conflict and hope'.

Pentycross has been described as 'an affectionate husband, an engaging preceptor, an agreeable companion, a faithful friend, and an eminent minister'.[30] He was certainly faithful to the call of God on his life, preferring to stay among his flock at Wallingford, rather than remove to other situations of greater honour and profit. He served his church, with patience and determination, for thirty-four years for a pitiful remuneration, and though by no means a perfect man, persevered through good times and bad to the glory of God. In his own words, he outpreached, outprayed and outlived his enemies. His influence for good touched the lives of many, and he was instrumental in bringing about a reconciliation between John Wesley and Rowland Hill, two stalwart protagonists in the controversy over Arminianism and Calvinism. To the end of his days he was chaplain to the Earl of Selkirk.

He was not a prolific writer, but in the years 1774/5 he was the editor of the *Gospel Magazine* and wrote some of the leading articles in those volumes. Several years later he supported the *Theological Repository*, and in 1781 published a book of sermons, addressed to his parishioners. At different times, he wrote out several individual sermons, one of which had been preached before the Missionary Society in 1796, and he once published a poem.

Four clergymen, Thomas Wills, William Piercy, William Taylor and Cradock Glascott, were sent out in the summer of 1781 under the patronage of Lady Huntingdon to preach the gospel in towns and villages in different parts of England. As they preached they sent back regular reports to her ladyship about the success of their labours. These letters were collected and published the following year under the title *Extracts of the Journals of Several Ministers of the Gospel*, an interesting work that was edited by Pentycross. At the close of his preface, Pentycross unveils his support for the revival by remarking, 'Respecting the unworthy writer of this introduction (necessary, as the printer alleged, for someone) nothing but the obligations and dependency of his peculiar station, restrain him from not only prefacing these sheets, but heartily and universally joining in the labour they recite.'[31]

It was not in the study, however, but in the pulpit, where he felt at home and where his God-given abilities shone most brightly. Scott in his funeral sermon said he possessed talents of a peculiar kind.

[He] told you almost the thoughts of your heart; and led you to fear, that the eyes of the congregation would be turned upon you. Yes, his words constrained your consciences, in some instances to say, 'Thou art the man.' You often could not help saying in your hearts, 'This is true; this is good counsel; this is meant in love, though I feel disposed to resent it. It would be well for me, if I complied with this admonition.' ...

I would earnestly entreat you [continues Scott] to remember your deceased minister; and in your retired hours to dwell on the recollection of the fervour, with which he has, in many instances, recommended your souls, and the souls of your dear children and relatives, to the special blessing of God our Saviour.[32]

His preaching was not personal, but familiar, impressive and searching. He owned a brilliant and fervid imagination, with which he was able to describe in great detail a subject he wanted to unfold, and then, with force and originality, use it to strike the consciences of his hearers. These sudden appeals to the heart often took his flock by surprise, and caused them to embrace the truth he was expounding. More often than not he preached with a 'glowing fervour of zeal and love, and an eloquence formed upon the peculiar traits of several distinguished orators, whom he admired and insensibly imitated in his youth'. One example will suffice.

'Principalities and powers of darkness,' the gospel of Jesus Christ defies you. That august and holy matron, the church universal, shakes her head at you; and, with 'him who sits in the heavens', laughs you to scorn. Annihilate Christianity! Try first to depopulate heaven, and expunge creation. Your poison shall become medicine to the church; your rage against it shall be its propagation, its perfection, its glory. Your earthquakes, that overthrow mountains, shall only fill up valleys, to make an immense level for the grand millennial car of the Son of God.[33]

In and out of the pulpit he was always deeply aware of his own unworthiness. His friends could testify that they never heard any contemporary express himself in such humiliating terms and with the most ardent sincerity of heart. It was this lowliness of spirit that kept him teachable before men and dependent on God, and was the foundation for the success he enjoyed.

There is no more fitting way to close this biography than with the tribute paid to him by Scott in his funeral sermon preached before the Wallingford congregation.

Chapter 5

He was in his youth brought to know the divine Saviour, and to trust, love and serve him. He entered the ministry from proper motives and for right purposes; which alas! is but seldom the case. He was stationed among you at an early period of his ministry. He had no attractions respecting emolument, for continuing among you. He possessed talents of a peculiar kind, and well suited to procure him situations, which to a worldly mind, would have appeared more eligible. But, he had here a large field for his ministry; a good opening, as he judged, to win souls: and he chose to abide with his flock; and accordingly has filled up the important, arduous and honourable station of a parochial minister among you for more than thirty years. Yes, my brethren, he was willing to spend and be spent among you.[34]

Endnotes

1 *Evangelical Magazine*, November 1808, p. 454.
2 **L.E. Elliot-Binns,** *The Early Evangelicals: A Religious and Social Study* (Greenwich, Seabury Press, 1955), p. 360.
3 **A.C.H. Seymour,** *The Life and Times of Selina Countess of Huntingdon* (Stoke-on-Trent, Tentmaker, 2000 reprint), vol. 2, p. 44n.
4 **Duncan Crookes Tovey (editor),** *The Letters of Thomas Gray* (London, George Bell & Sons, 1900–12), vol. 3, p. 178.
5 **Seymour,** *Countess of Huntingdon*, vol. 2, p. 44n.
6 **William Jones,** *Memoir of Rowland Hill* (London, Henry G. Bohn, 1853), pp. 66–69.
7 **John Wesley,** *The Works of John Wesley* (Grand Rapids, Baker Books House, 1998 reprint), vol. 4, p. 7.
8 **Seymour,** *Countess of Huntingdon*, vol. 2, p. 44n.
9 **Wesley,** *Works*, vol. 3, p. 381.
10 **Henry Venn,** *The Letters of Henry Venn* (Edinburgh, Banner of Truth Trust, 1993 reprint), pp. 223–224.
11 **Seymour,** *Countess of Huntingdon*, vol. 2, p. 65.
12 *Ibid.*
13 *Ibid.*, p. 45.
14 *Ibid.*
15 *Evangelical Magazine*, November 1808, p. 458.
16 **Seymour,** *Countess of Huntingdon*, vol. 2, p. 46.
17 *Ibid.*, p. 64.

18 *Ibid.*

19 Jones, *Rowland Hill*, p. 108.

20 Edward W. Broome, *Rowland Hill: Preacher and Wit* (London, Cassell, Petter, Galpin & Co., 1881), p. 32.

21 *Evangelical Magazine*, November 1808, p. 458n.

22 *Ibid.*, December 1808, p. 497.

23 William Romaine, *The Whole Works of William Romaine* (London, B. Blake, 1837), p. 653.

24 *Evangelical Magazine*, December 1808, p. 498n.

25 Seymour, *Countess of Huntingdon*, vol. 2, p. 48n.

26 *Evangelical Magazine*, December 1808, p. 499.

27 Wesley, *Works*, vol. 4, pp. 439, 474.

28 *Evangelical Magazine*, December 1808, pp. 500–501.

29 Thomas Scott, *The Duty and Advantage of Remembering Deceased Ministers* (Buckingham, 1808), p. 26.

30 *Evangelical Magazine*, December 1808, p. 502.

31 Thomas Pentycross (editor), *Extracts of the Journals of Several Ministers of the Gospel* (London, 1782), p. iv.

32 Scott, *The Duty and Advantage of Remembering Deceased Ministers*, pp. 13–14, 15.

33 *Evangelical Magazine*, December 1808, p. 503.

34 Scott, *The Duty and Advantage of Remembering Deceased Ministers*, p. 31.

Index

A

Adlington, Lancashire   107
America   10, 23, 54, 136
American War of Independence   53
Analogy   142
Anglican Church   26, 134
Argument in Defence of the
   Exclusive Right Claimed
   by the Colonies to Tax
   Themselves, An   51
Arminian Magazine   42
Arminianism   23, 42, 183, 186
Armitage, William   75
Aston Sandford,
   Buckinghamshire   185

B

Bacon, John (the elder)   130, 131
Baliol, John   62
Barnstaple, Devon   8, 10, 15, 27
Barrow, Ann   82
Barrow, Samuel   82
Barry, Edward   182
Bath   15, 17, 19, 45, 47, 77, 175,
   176, 179, 180
Baxter, Richard   155
Bayley, Cornelius   134
Bedminster, Bristol   37
Bennet, John   8, 15, 16, 17, 22, 30
Benson, Joseph   35, 46, 131, 136
Berridge, John   119, 171
Berwick, Shropshire   66, 72
Betton Strange, Shrewsbury   62
Bideford, Devon   13, 15, 22
Birmingham   117

Blackburne, Francis   100
Boden, James   80
Brickdale, Matthew   45
Brighton   65, 66
Bristol   32, 36, 37, 38, 39, 40, 42, 43,
   44, 46, 49, 53, 54, 55, 56, 77, 171,
   172
Bristol Dispensary   57
Bristol Grammar School   39
Bristol Society for Relief and
   Discharge of Persons Confined
   for Small Debts, The   50
Britain, Jonathan   47, 49
Brown, James   39, 43, 44, 46, 47
Brynsworthy, Devon   10, 13, 14
Buckingham   101, 102, 103,
   104, 105
Bull, John   54
Bullock Smithy (Hazel Grove)   112,
   115, 134
Bunyan, John   132
Burscoe, John   105, 106
Buxton, Derbyshire   80

C

Calm Address to our American
   Colonies   51
Calvinism   49, 50, 112, 181, 186
Cambridge   93, 94, 95, 96, 97, 98,
   99, 100, 101, 170
Camelford, Cornwall   13, 26
Campbell, Willielma, Lady
   Glenorchy   79, 80, 81
Cannon, John   36
Castleton, Derbyshire   105

Catterick, Yorkshire 94, 95
Charity schools 128, 129
Cheadle, Staffordshire 80
Cheshire 74, 78, 79, 82, 84
Cheshire Congregational
  Union 82
Chester 75, 83, 105, 106, 113, 124, 127
Chichester, Sussex 176, 179
Christ Church, Macclesfield 115, 116, 123, 125, 128, 134, 153
Christ Church, Oxford 39
Christ's Hospital 166
Christian Monitor, The 92
Christian Strife, The 45
Church of England 19, 35, 52, 55, 103, 113, 115, 118, 125, 134, 135, 155, 156, 158, 170
City Road Chapel, London 109
Claggett, Bishop Nicholas 17, 18
Clarke, John 56
Clay, Elizabeth 73
Clayton, John 178
Cleckheaton, Yorkshire 119
Coetlogon, Charles de 97, 101, 135, 170
Collection of Psalms and Hymns and Spiritual Songs, for the Use of Christians of Every Denomination, A 127
Colston, Edward 40
Congleton, Cheshire 78, 82, 141
Cornwall 8, 10, 13, 15, 17, 18, 21, 22, 25, 30
Cory, John 17

Coughlan, Lawrence 115
Coventry 85
Cowper, William 101

D

Dawson, William 93
Death of a Great and Good Man Lamented and Improved, The 56
Debat, Daniel 43
Deloraine, Earl of 36
Devon 13, 14, 25
Dingley, Rebecca 15
Dissenters 17, 25, 47, 56, 73, 80, 103, 117, 125, 126, 155, 157, 158, 178, 182
Doddridge, Philip 11, 19, 20
Drayton, Shropshire 74, 79
Dublin 109
Dunkerley, Daniel 79
Duty and Advantage of Remembering Deceased Ministers, The 185

E

Elegiac Thoughts 153
Eliot, Honor 15
Elswick, Lancashire 77
Encouragements to Exertion in the Spread of the Gospel 82
Essay on Fatalism 136
Evans, Caleb 32, 35, 37, 43, 44, 50, 51, 52, 56, 57, 58
Evans, William 82
Everton, Bedfordshire 171

Index

Exeter   10, 13, 18
Exeter College, Oxford   10
*Extracts of the Journals of Several
Ministers of the Gospel*   186

F

Felix Farley's Bristol Journal   35,
37, 46, 58
Fenwicke, Edward   36
Fletcher, John 51, 52, 55, 70, 71, 84,
117, 118
Foundery, The, London   49
Francis, Molly   35
Fremington, Devon   8
Furly, Samuel   12, 22, 23, 26, 27

G

Gardiner, Colonel   11
Garstang, Lancashire   76
Gawcott, Buckinghamshire   102
George, William   45
Glascott, Cradock   186
Gloucester   35, 44, 129
Gloucester, Bishop of   35
*God's Choice the Best for his
People*   133
Goode, John   103
Goode, William   102
Gospel Magazine   186
Gould, Rowland   124
Gray, Thomas   170
Green, Bishop   102
Grigg, Peter   43
Gwennap, Cornwall   16
Gwynne, Sally   34

H

Handel   121
Hanley, Staffordshire   78, 80, 81
*Happiness of Dying in the Lord,
The*   111
Hardy, Elizabeth   37
Harriot, Rachel   104
Hart, Richard   39
Hastings, Selina, Countess of
Huntingdon   36, 40, 43, 45, 46,
47, 65, 71, 81, 84, 103, 104, 115,
116, 173, 175, 176, 177, 178, 180,
182, 186
Haynes, D.S.   46
Henbury Hall   113
Henry, Matthew   75
Hervey, James 10, 13, 14, 15, 22, 27
Hewson, Thomas   106, 107, 124
Highworth, Wiltshire   175
Hill, Charles   19
Hill, Richard   69, 70
Hill, Rowland   37, 44, 50, 52, 53,
55, 56, 57, 78, 79, 84, 96, 116, 169,
171, 180, 186
Horley, Surrey   173
Hot Wells, Bristol   36
Howard, General   72
Huntingdon, Countess of. *See*
Hastings, Selina, Countess of
Huntingdon
Hutton Rudby, Yorkshire   92, 131

I

Independents   140
Ingleby Arncliffe, Yorkshire   90

Ireland 35

J

Jacobstow, Jacobstow 10
Jebb, John 100
Johnson, Samuel 52
Jones, John 35
Jones, Thomas 74
Jortin, John 127
Joss, Torial 75
Joy, Thomas 96

K

Key to the Prophecies 90, 139
Kidderminster, Worcestershire 39
Kilkhampton, Cornwall 14, 17
Kingswood School, Bristol 34, 35, 46
Knowle, Bristol 38

L

Lancashire 74, 84
Lancaster, Lancashire 76, 77
Laneast, Cornwall 8
Lavington, Bishop George 19, 20, 21
Leaver, William 17
Lee, John 111, 149, 150, 151
Leeds 52, 71, 112
Leicester 70, 71, 138
Lewes, Sussex 179
Lindsey, Theophilus 94, 95, 96, 100
Lloyd-Jones, Martyn 5
Lock Chapel 135

London 10, 18, 32, 36, 49, 50, 65, 66, 75, 76, 97, 103, 104, 109, 115, 116, 121, 135, 136, 146, 148, 151, 166, 173, 180, 182
London Chronicle 38
Lucas, Penelope 15
Luther, Martin 116

M

Macclesfield 78, 82, 90, 92, 97, 104, 105, 106, 108, 110, 111, 112, 114, 115, 116, 118, 119, 121, 127, 134, 136, 140, 143, 149, 153, 159
Maclardie, Aeneas 121
Maddern, John 35
Madeley 51, 70, 71, 84, 117
Magor, Matthew 49
Manchester 72, 77, 79, 112, 134, 135, 153
Marazion, Cornwall 18
Marhamchurch, Cornwall 17
Market Drayton, Shropshire 73, 74
Markham, Bishop William 113, 124
Marriage Honourable, Whoredom Damnable 113
Marriot, William 178
Marriott, Thomas 178
Mather, Alexander 156
Matlock, Derbyshire 80, 81, 82
Maurice, William 78
Maxfield, Thomas 17, 41, 42
Meditations among the Tombs 14
Merchant Taylors' School, London 32

Meredith, Sir William   113
Meriton, John   16
Metcalfe, John   143
Methodism   17, 21, 90, 102, 110, 112, 113, 124, 126, 170
Methodists   15, 17, 43, 47, 74, 109, 110, 111, 113, 124, 125, 126, 156, 157, 170
Middlewich, Cheshire   78, 82
Milner, Joseph   100
Minden, Battle of   62
Moravians   22, 43
More, Hannah   52

N

Nantwich, Cheshire   77, 82
Narrative of the Whole of his Proceedings Relative to Jonathan Britain   48
Newcastle-under-Lyme, Staffordshire   77, 80
Newgate Prison, Bristol   37, 38, 42, 45, 48, 50
Newport, Shropshire   74, 75
Newton, John   69, 72, 73, 101, 102
Nightingale, Joseph   153
Noble, John   93, 96
North Tamerton, Cornwall   8
Northallerton, Yorkshire   90, 93
Northwich, Cheshire   78, 82

O

Oakes, Edward   131
Office and Duty of a Minister of the Gospel, The   114

Oldham Street Methodist Chapel, Manchester   134
Ollerton, Shropshire   75
Olney, Buckinghamshire   69, 70, 101
Original Sacred Hymns   12, 23
Osmotherly, Yorkshire   114
Oswestry, Shropshire   80
Ote Hall, Sussex   65
Oxford   20, 21, 34, 39, 66, 170
Oxford University   121

P

Paine, Thomas   136
Paley, William   100
Park Green   121, 129
Parkinson, John   35
Pawson, John   49
Pembroke College, Cambridge   169, 170
Penryn, Cornwall   16
Pentycross, Mrs (Thomas's wife)   175
Pentycross, Thomas   97
Perfectionism   42
Piercy, William   186
Pilgrim's Progress, The   132
Pine, William   47, 51
Plea for Religion and the Sacred Writings, A   136
Plymouth   21
Porteus, Bishop Beilby   124, 125
Powys, Thomas   66
Prayer in Commemoration of Bristol's Benefactors   45

Preston 76
Price, Thomas 101
Priestley, Joseph 95, 99, 136

R

Raikes, Robert 129
Ramsden Bellhouse, Essex 101
Redruth, Cornwall 17, 21
Reece, Richard 145, 151
Rigge, Dr 47
Robinson, Robert
(Cambridge) 99
Robinson, Thomas 100
Roche, Cornwall 22
Roe, Charles 104, 107, 109, 115,
122, 131
Roe, Frances 111
Roe, Hester Ann 107, 108, 111,
123, 131
Roe, James 107
Roe, Robert 107, 109
Roe, Thomas 105
Rogers, James 109, 111
Rogers, Martha 111
Romaine, William 36, 65, 66, 67,
69, 75, 102, 118, 119, 127, 173,
177, 178, 181
Rouquet (née Cannon,
Rouquet's second wife), Mary 36
Rouquet (née Fenwicke,
Rouquet's first wife), Sarah 36
Rouquet, Anthony 32
Rowson, James 106
Ryland, John 117
Ryle, John 121

S

Sabbath 20
Sackville, Lord George 62
Sacred Literature 135
St Edmund Hall, Oxford 74, 170
St Gennys, Cornwall 8, 10, 11, 13,
15, 16, 17, 18, 21, 22, 25
St George's, Bristol 39
St George's, Hanover Square 36
St Giles, Reading 48
St Ives, Cornwall 17, 21
St James's Church, Manchester 134
St John's College, Cambridge 93
St John's College, Oxford 32
St Luke's, London 36
St Mary's, Wallingford 173, 176,
182
St Michael's, Macclesfield 105,
124, 126
St Michael's Hill, Bristol 40, 42, 47
St Michael's Mount, Cornwall 17
St Nicholas, Bristol 44
St Paul's Cathedral 100
St Peter's Church, Bristol 56
St Peter's Hospital, Bristol 44, 46,
55, 57
St Stephen's Church, Bristol 44
St Werburgh's, Bristol 44, 46, 56
Sandhurst, Gloucester 35
Scorton, Yorkshire 93, 94
Scotland 97
Scott, Elizabeth 62
Scott, Richard 62
Scott, Thomas (Bible
commentator) 93

Index

Scott, Thomas (Rector of Aston
  Sandford)   185
Scott, Thomas (younger son of
  Bible commentator)   102
*Second Check to Civil
  Antinomianism, A*   52
Select Psalms and Hymns   127
Sellon, Walter   35
Serle, Thomas   17
Seven Years' War   38, 62
Sheffield   133, 142
Shrewsbury   62, 65, 66, 69
Shropshire   66, 67, 73, 74, 79, 84,
  111, 153
Silvester, Moses   75
Simpson, Ann (née Waldy,
  Simpson's first wife)   110, 111
Simpson, Ann (Simpson's
  daughter by his first
  marriage)   111, 149
Simpson, Anne (Simpson's
  mother)   92
Simpson, David (Simpson's son)
  132, 148, 151
Simpson, Elizabeth (née Davey,
  Simpson's second wife)   144, 145,
  146, 147, 148, 149, 150, 156
Simpson, Elizabeth (Simpson's
  daughter by his second
  marriage)   146
Simpson, Ralph (Simpson's
  father)   92
Socinianism   75
*Some Particulars of the Life and
  Death of Jonathan Britain*   47

Stafford   80
Staffordshire   72, 74, 77, 78, 84
Stage Entertainments   135
Stillingfleet, James   119
Stock Harward   100
Stockport   78, 82, 134
Stoke-on-Trent   76
Stone, Staffordshire   72, 77
Stourbridge Grammar School   141
Sunday Schools   102, 129, 132, 180
Surrey Chapel, London   180, 184
Symes, Richard   44

T

Talbot, William   48
Tawstock, Devon   19
Taxation no Tyranny   52
Taylor, Joseph   141
Taylor, William   186
Terrick, Richard   100
Thatched House Society,
  London   50
Theological Repository   186
Thomson, Captain   29
Thornton, John   123
Tidings from Wallingford   184
Tiverton College, Wales   136
*Token of Respect to the
  Memory of the Late
  Rev. J. Rouquet, A*   56
Toleration Act, The   115, 116, 118
Tomkins, Henry   18
Toplady, Augustus   112, 135
Townley, James   153
Treneglos, Cornwall   17

Tresmere, Cornwall 8
Trevanion, Grace 15
Trevanion, Sir Nicholas 15
Trevecca College 39
Trowbridge, Wiltshire 47
Tunbridge Wells, Kent 103, 104, 115
Turner, John 30

U

Ubley, Somerset 43
Ulverston, Cumbria 76
Unitarians 77
Unitas Fratrum 22
Unwin, Mary 101
Unwin, William 100
Uttoxeter, Staffordshire 77

V

Venn, Henry 66, 67, 68, 70, 77, 84, 116
Vernon, Elizabeth 74

W

Walcot, Anne 180
Wales 114, 136
Walker, Samuel 8
Wallingford, Oxfordshire 166, 173, 174, 175, 176, 177, 178, 179, 180, 181, 182, 184, 185, 187
Walpole, Horatio 168
Walsh, Thomas 37
Warbstow, Cornwall 17
Warburg, Germany 62
Waters Upton, Shropshire 153

Watts, Isaac 12, 141
Webb, Captain Thomas 43
Week St Mary, Cornwall 18, 30
Wem, Shropshire 111
Wesley, Charles 15, 16, 18, 34, 36
Wesley, John 17, 18, 21, 26, 34, 36, 37, 45, 49, 51, 52, 54, 104, 109, 111, 121, 134, 156, 173, 184, 186
Wesleyan Missionary Society 153, 178
Wesleys 8, 12, 18, 34, 51
West Harptree, Somerset 39, 43, 46
West, John 102
Westminster 179
Whitaker, John 90, 129
Whitefield, George 5, 8, 13, 15, 16, 21, 22, 23, 28, 32, 46, 71, 75, 77, 83, 170, 171
Whitridge, John 80
Williams, Edward 80
Williams, Joseph 39
Wills, Bishop Edward 43
Wills, Thomas 179, 182, 186
Wilson, Job 78
Wistanswick, Shropshire 75
Wollerton, Shropshire 73, 74, 79
Worn-out Preachers' Fund 178
Wotton-under-Edge, Gloucestershire 180

Y

Yarm, Yorkshire 110, 111